Anand Teltumbde is a leading public intellectual and is known for his critical insights on many a contemporary issue. A civil rights activist of long standing, he is currently General Secretary of the Committee for Protection of Democratic Rights (CPDR). He is also associated with the All India Forum for Rights to Education (AIFRTE), which is spearheading the movement for common school system, as a member of its Presidium and many other Peoples' movements. He wrote a monthly column 'Margin Speak' for a decade before switching it to 'Outlook' after his release on bail in November 2022. He writes another column "The Unquiet Republic" for The Wire. He also regularly contributes to other progressive journals, portals, and most English newspapers. Some of his recent books are *Whither Human Rights in India* (Penguin, 2025), *Caste Con Census* (Navayana, 2025), *The Cell and The Soul: A Prison Memor* (Bloomsburry, 2025), and *Iconoclast: A Reflective Biography of Babasaheb Ambedkar* (Penguin, 2024). He is widely translated into most Indian languages. Professionally, he was trained in Engineering and Management and held top management positions in the corporate world. After his corporate stint, he was invited by IIT, Kharagpur where he taught Business Management for six years before switching to Goa Institute of Management as Senior Professor, where he set up a Big Data Analtics (BDA) Centre and pioneered a PG Course in Management with based on BDA.

Dalits
and the Indian Constitution

Anand Teltumbde

SPEAKING
TIGER

SPEAKING TIGER BOOKS
125A, Ground Floor, Shahpur Jat, near Asiad Village,
New Delhi 110049

First published by Speaking Tiger Books 2025

ISBN: 978-93-6336-555-1
eISBN: 978-93-6336-397-7

10 9 8 7 6 5 4 3 2 1

Typeset in Garamond Premier Pro by
SŪRYA, New Delhi

CONTENTS

INTRODUCTION

Has India's Constitution Fulfilled its Emancipatory Promises?

Harsh Mander

We thought it fitting to invite India's highly regarded scholar Anand Teltumbde—also one who recently served time as a prisoner of conscience—to write the closing book in the series of eleven short treatises by leading scholars on the ideas of free India's constitution. In this series, we have looked at how the constitution was imagined, debated and written; its understanding of secularism, socialism and democracy; and its foundational pledges of justice, liberty, equality, fraternity, federalism and the scientific temper. We requested Teltumbde to reflect on what the constitution has meant for India's most dispossessed peoples, and how much it has contributed to helping access their rights to a life of dignity and hope.

His conclusions are sobering, scathing and unsparing.

Teltumbde sees an immense gap between the vision laid out in the Preamble and the realities of India's present. "Liberty is under attack. Economic inequality is worse now than it was even under colonial rule. Fraternity has been shredded by rising communal hatred and growing caste consciousness under the revivalist Hindutva movement. Justice—social, economic, and political—remains elusive. The very foundation of our democracy feels dangerously fragile".

Teltumbde argues that we should not be constrained from constructively critiquing the constitution because at this moment its very survival is gravely threatened by the Hindutva project of dismantling and rewriting the constitution to establish a Hindu Rashtra. With Ambedkar, he is convinced that a Hindu Rashtra would be the greatest calamity for India. Unlike the critique of the constitution of the reactionary far-right, he affirms the emancipatory promise of the Preamble—liberty, equality, fraternity, and justice. Yet, he sees these as values the Constitution pledged but has failed to deliver. "Yes", he says boldly, "the Constitution is flawed...but dismantling it without first building a genuinely democratic and pro-people alternative would be to destroy the last remaining legal and moral structure within which the struggle for justice can still be waged".

The Gravest Betrayals of the Constitution are Arguably of Dalits

His treatise focuses specifically on Dalits, who have for millennia been oppressed by structures of caste, and barred from education and dignified work. But they apply more generally to all oppressed and marginalised communities who constitute the Indian republic.

Teltumbde observes that on the one hand, perhaps Dalits feel the greatest emotional connection among all Indians to the constitution. This is because its writing was led by Dr Babasaheb Ambedkar who they venerate for leading the struggles for their liberation from the centuries-old bondages of caste.

Yet, he believes that the Constitution has failed resoundingly in fulfilling its emancipatory promise for Dalits, arguably more than for any other community. It has contributed to the rise of a small Dalit middle-class. But this small class shares with the large mass of Dalits only "a history but not a present". The overwhelming majority of Dalits continue to endure the caste stigma and oppression that has been their fate for millennia, living in "a vast, submerged reality of suffering and despair".

Dalits, he points out, form a quarter of India's population, if we include Dalit Christians and Dalit Muslims. Their population, exceeding 320 million, would make them the third-largest "nation" in the world, larger than the combined population of 150 of the least populous countries on the planet. However, their wide dispersal across the country has meant that—like Muslims—they rarely form a numerical majority.

Teltumbde rejects the premise of some Hindutva intellectuals that the British rule created caste. But, he avers that colonial rule fundamentally transformed caste. Before the British, caste was a dynamic, localized system. The British began counting and documenting caste. This, quoting Arjun Appadurai, didn't just describe caste—it *produced* it as a rigid, bureaucratized, institutionalized hierarchy, solidifying boundaries that were previously contextual and fluid. This colonial approach, Teltumbde states, continues to reverberate in India's social and political life.

He also observes that paradoxically, colonial rule also opened some emancipatory pathways for Dalits outside the rigid caste structures of Hindu kingdoms. They found non-caste employment for the first time in the military and railways, and were able to access education and stable employment. Babasaheb himself was the son of a British military soldier.

Teltumbde importantly reminds us that until Gandhiji, the Indian National Congress- dominated as it was by English-educated elites, landlords, and emerging capitalists—tended to steer clear of calling for reforms in caste, untouchability and the status of women. It later made space for moderate reforms such as widow remarriage, child marriage, and even the abolition of untouchability, but never the annihilation of caste. It was Mahatma Gandhi who brought fighting untouchability into the core of the Congress agenda from 1916 onward. Particularly impactful was his movement for Dalit temple entry.

The limitation of Gandhiji's approach was that while he and the Congress looked at untouchability as a moral question and a social sin to be atoned for by caste Hindus, they did not frame it as a systemic injustice that required political solutions. This conflicted with Ambedkar's demands for separate electorates. Gandhiji went on a fast unto death against separate electorates because he feared this would break Hindu unity and also encourage the Muslim League to make a similar demand. The compromise in the Poona Pact of 1932 was for reserved seats for Dalits within the general electorate rather than separate electorates. Ambedkar was dissatisfied with this because he was convinced that Dalits formed a separate community from caste Hindus like the Muslims, and therefore only separate electorates would protect their political and social interests. Gandhiji followed this with a temple entry movement which incensed the conservative Hindu, but this still was not a movement for political empowerment of the Dalits.

The Constitution Abolished Untouchability but Not Caste

Teltumbde regards as the central flaw of the constitutional arrangements for Dalits to be that once again it stressed the abolition of untouchability rather than the annihilation of caste. The Constituent Assembly was dominated by upper-caste, Western-educated elites, landlords, and capitalists, with limited participation from workers, peasants, or marginalized groups especially Dalits and Adivasis. Dr Ambedkar, a Dalit, was appointed to chair the Drafting Committee. Under his leadership, many provisions for advancing Dalit equity found their way into the constitution, including the bans on untouchability and forced labour, and reservations in public employment and education. However, contrary to what Ambedkar had so forcefully advocated for in the 1930s, it did not outlaw caste and provide for separate Dalit electorates.

In the debates in the Constituent Assembly, some members opposed caste-based reservations as incompatible with liberal democratic ideals and pointed to the risks of deepening social fragmentation. However, the alternate view prevailed, that legal equality without structural interventions like affirmative actions would be insufficient to dismantle entrenched caste hierarchies.

The Assembly unanimously voted for declaring untouchability unconstitutional and a punishable offense. Some members did question how untouchability could be eradicated without addressing the root problem—caste itself. This called to memory the fundamental disagreement between Babasaheb and Gandhiji. Gandhiji saw untouchability as a distortion of the caste system; Babasaheb insisted that untouchability was intrinsic to the caste system, and the caste system to the Hindu faith. Therefore untouchability could not be ended without ending caste.

In the assembly, Pramatha Ranjan Thakur, great-grandson of Harichand Thakur, the founder of the Matua sect (the first Dalit reform movement) for instance, argued: "I do not understand how you can abolish untouchability without abolishing the very caste system. Untouchability is nothing but the symptom of the disease, namely, the caste system... Unless we can do away with the caste system altogether there is no use tinkering with the problem of untouchability superficially."

A couple of other members raised similar objections. But Teltumbde points to Ambedkar's telling silence in the Constituent Assembly on the critique that untouchability could not be abolished without dismantling caste—a position that he had so passionately espoused for most of his adult life—and describes this as a strategic compromise.

Overruling the few dissenting voices, the Constituent Assembly unanimously passed the resolution to abolish untouchability and criminalize its practice. This resulted in Article 17 which states: "Untouchability is abolished and its practice in any form is forbidden. The enforcement of any disability arising out of untouchability shall be an offence punishable in accordance with law." Hansa Mehta, one of the two women members of the drafting committee called this "the greatest thing that we have done," a move that "posterity will be very, very proud of."

Was India's Failure to Abolish Untouchability a "Failure Foretold"?

Pointing to extensive evidence of the persistence of untouchability and violent caste discrimination in contemporary India, Teltumbde wonders at what he describes as a "failure foretold". "How could the persistence of caste in independent India not have been foreseen by the galaxy of 300-odd stalwarts in the Constituent Assembly?" he asks. Gandhiji's position that untouchability was a moral perversion, not intrinsic to Hinduism, and "his defence of the ideal of *varna*, albeit spiritualized and purged of birth-based inequality" is well-known. (Toward the end of his life, Gandhiji had spoken more directly against caste discrimination). But why did Jawaharlal Nehru, a self-avowed modernist, not challenge the caste system more vocally? He did recognise caste to be a social evil and called instead for scientific temper and rationalism. However, Teltumbde observes that he remained politically cautious indicating a deeper political calculus. Possibly his fear was that caste was so pivotal an organising principle of Hindu life that directly attacking it might destabilise the emerging republic. And Nehru was dealing with a significant section of the Congress leadership that was socially conservative and had internalized caste hierarchies.

Teltumbde also points to the irony of the anxiety of many Dalit leaders that the abolition of caste might jeopardise their constitutional safeguards of reservations. Caste embedded itself further in the new republic with its intersections with class. The lower castes transformed into a rural proletariat. The erstwhile Shudras became a class of rich farmers, which "not only accumulated economic power but also appropriated the ideological mantle of Brahmanism from the former upper-caste landlords, (whom they displaced) deploying it to dominate, discipline, and violently suppress Dalits". This, he observes, erupted from time to time in brutal atrocities. The constitutional order that formally guaranteed rights was unequal to the challenge of dismantling the caste structure within which such violence and largescale discrimination continued unabated. He points, likewise, to the continuance of the most abysmal forms of caste discrimination like manual scavenging and bonded labour.

Teltumbde concludes that despite Article 17, untouchability remains entrenched in everyday life. The problem, he says, is that the constitution banned untouchability but did not abolish caste itself. In this way it allowed the social and institutional structures that sustain caste-based inequities, discrimination, violence and exclusions to persist. The problem is further escalated because the state institutions created to enforce the law—the police, judiciary, and bureaucracy—are themselves deeply stained by caste prejudice and even hatred. Their routine refusal to register cases, downgrading of offences, delays in trial, and sympathy for dominant caste perpetrators are not random failures; they become inevitable when caste endures and strengthens.

"When the state machinery shares the worldview of those who uphold caste hierarchy, constitutional guarantees offer little relief to Dalits. Legal prohibitions, he explains, have inevitably failed because the underlying caste structure remains intact.

This is further inflamed in the current BJP Hindutva regime. "Revivalist Hindu nationalism glorifies traditional social order, providing ideological cover for caste hierarchy. Open display of caste markers, segregation in temples and villages, and caste-based mobilization have become widespread. Social media has further amplified these assertions. The state, aligning with dominant caste interests, often protects perpetrators and grants them impunity".

The result, as Teltumbde documents, is caste having become more visible, aggressive, and socially sanctioned than before. He sticks his head out to suggest that "*India today is arguably more casteized than ever*"(my italics). In these ways, constitutional ideals are routinely subverted by social reality and state complicity.

Political Representation Has Done Little to Deliver Substantive Empowerment

Teltumbde is underwhelmed in his assessment of the contributions of political reservations for Dalits. This is not different from the global experience that while political reservations increase descriptive representation, they rarely deliver substantive empowerment. In the way political representation is designed in India's electoral syatem, with Dalits rarely in a majority even in constituencies reserved for Dalits, they are forced by electoral compulsions into multi-caste alliances. The rotation of reserved seats incentivizes short-term patronage. Party affiliations further dilute accountability, shifting loyalty from community to party. The dependence of Dalit candidates on intermediaries—brokers, fixers, party workers—to access state power through those with money or influence, renders representation hollow for many Dalits. Overall, Teltumbde tells us, research shows that reservations do not systematically translate into pro-Dalit policy outcomes.

Even more gravely, he avers that political reservation has resulted in what he calls the "domestication" of Dalit leadership: instead of confronting caste power, it has been absorbed by it. His dire conclusion is that political reservations have enabled the emergence of Dalit elites without enabling Dalit emancipation. Also, in the first-past-the-post electoral system, reservations are less instruments of empowerment of the community and more as seeking their buy-in to those who enjoy political, social and economic power.

He believes that instead, a system of proportional representation based on vote shares alone would prevent the marginalization of smaller or dispersed communities. It would help convert caste and community identities into political interest groups, and with less need for identity-based reservations, it could gradually support the project of caste annihilation. Unlike reservations which require statutory backing, proportional representation could organically enable minority inclusion.

Caste Quotas in Educational Institutions and Public Employment

Teltumbde also examines closely the impacts of caste quotas in educational institutions and public employment. In the Constituent Assembly debates, it was Dr. Ambedkar who most forcefully argued for these as reparative justice to redress centuries of caste-based oppression and exclusion, for a people who historically "were not only not allowed to enter the public services but were also prohibited from pursuing ordinary education". He also argued that reservations were essential to allow SCs entry into administration and political life, so they could protect their rights and assert their voice in governance.

Other members supported him. In a tenor similar to Ambedkar's, K. Santhanam said that reservation for SCs was "not a privilege but an act of compensation for centuries of oppression and humiliation." KM Munshi warned the members that if constitutional safeguards are not put in place, dominant castes would continue to monopolize opportunities, thereby reproducing structural inequality. Jaipal Singh, speaking for tribal communities, predicted discerningly: "Unless they get reservations, they will never catch up with the rest of India." RK Sidhva added that education was key to social mobility, and reservations were a matter of justice, not charity.

But we also heard in the Constituent Assembly opposition to affirmative action on grounds that we continue to hear repeated decades later, of merit and efficiency being trumped by quotas. HV Kamath, for instance, said, "We should not sacrifice efficiency at the altar of social justice." RV Dhulekar said that merit and equality before law should be paramount. But the Assembly in the end supported reservations, providing for these in Articles 15(4), 16(4), and 335 of the Constitution.

Evaluating the impact of these, Teltumbde observes that reservation policies in educational institutions and public employment have the merit that these at least touch directly upon the material conditions of Dalit life unlike most other provisions in the Indian Constitution. Educational and job quotas have done more to foster a more egalitarian society than political reservations. For Dalits, pathways for upward economic mobility were barred for centuries. These pathways, Teltumbde observes, were opened potentially by affirmative action in education and public employment. These have, despite limitations, expanded Dalit presence in professions that were traditionally barred to them. They have enhanced economic security but broken through social hierarchies.

Yet, formulated as remedies for "backwardness" of these castes, Teltumbde believes that this framing constructs Dalits as though they were intrinsically deficient. This has reinforced casteist prejudices that Dalits are an inferior people deserving possibly of sympathy but not rights, and that they are being unfairly elevated by a state driven by vote-bank politics. Second, Dalits are themselves often made to feel that they are undeserving or second-rate. "What was originally conceived as a measure of social justice thus becomes a marker of social deficit".

Answering the critics of education and job quotas, Teltumbde articulates a profound social truth that reservations were not necessitated by any intrinsic deficiency among Dalits. These were impelled by the failings of Indian society, which continues to be hostile to the ideal of equality. Reservations are not a recompense for Dalit backwardness, but a corrective measure for societal deficiencies and entrenched caste prejudices. "It is not Dalit individuals who must 'catch up' with society, but the social order itself that must expunge its caste biases and catch up with the ideals of a modern, egalitarian polity". The state, through reservations, is not extending undue favours to a minority but is "disciplining a historically unjust majority".

The educational and occupational advancement of Dalits has often led to backlashes of resentment, anger and envy, and has been the trigger often for violence by dominant communities against "upstart" Dalits. Teltumbde also indicates sensitively the predicament of those who benefit from these quotas. They are excluded from middle-class networks because of the continuing prejudices of caste.

But at the same time, they are separated from their own caste communities, which continue to live in penury and want. This entails "profound psychological costs, including chronic anxiety, identity dissonance, and a persistent sense of inadequacy despite visible markers of success...reflecting a deep-drawn inferiority complex, inhibiting their ability to fully realize their potential".

Also, reservations rather than annihilating caste have, Teltumbde says, in some ways reinforced it within a framework of redress. This has led to a competitive hierarchy of entitlements, reproducing and embedding caste identities and caste tensions.

The massive gap in the educational opportunities for the elite and middle classes and the poor that existed at independence has only greatly widened. India failed to establish a Common School System, which ensured that, in Teltumbde's words, "educational access continued to follow social rank rather than democratic ideals". Public spending on education has stagnated at around 3% of GDP, far below the recommended 6% .

This has systematically pushed Dalits to the bottom of the educational hierarchy. Even in rural areas, the neo-rich dominant castes including the now landed Shudras—opt for private private schools, while poorly resourced and understaffed government schools remain the preserve of Dalit children. Therefore "Dalit children are trapped in a deteriorating government system that offers little mobility. The result is a harsh sorting mechanism: elites buy opportunity, while Dalits inherit deprivation, reinforcing caste hierarchy under the veneer of merit and market efficiency". Private schools and colleges, especially those offering English-medium education, overwhelmingly serve relatively better-off upper-caste elites. Private colleges increasingly dominate higher education, and these have no quotas. Although public universities have reservations, the domination of private education—entirely unaffordable for most Dalits—effectively nullifies the constitutional safeguards. This traps Dalit students in substandard institutions, rendering their academic foundations weak and severely limiting their future employment prospects.

Reservations in government employment have, in Teltumbde's assessment, delivered "meagre returns while imposing a disproportionate stigma". After all, the public sector where reservations apply covers barely about 4% of India's workforce, compared to 32% in China and 15–25% in countries of the Global North. He calculates that quotas translate into benefits for only about 0.6 percent of SCs and an even smaller proportion of STs. For this meagre support, Dalits are stigmatised and humiliated as "pampered" and dependent on state charity. And this tiny fraction of Dalits that access reservations face a hostile and discriminatory environment at work, confining them to low-impact roles and away from management and decision-making assignments. This, he says, turns the public sector into "a graveyard of Dalit aspirations".

He speaks for instance of academic spaces—traditionally the preserve of advantaged castes—being extremely reluctant to recruit Dalits as faculty, "treating them as intellectual interlopers rather than equals". In 2019, only 3.47% of professors and 0.7% of associate professors in forty central universities were SC/STs. In 2021, only 1.68% of IIT faculty and just 0.23% of IIMs were SC/ST.

How Indian Secularism "Constitutionalised" Caste

A particularly important and challenging section of the book is one that describes how the core foundation of "secularism" in the Indian constitution has been interpreted and implemented in ways that have only reinforced caste hierarchies and discrimination. Its core failure, according to Teltumbde, is that Indian secularism never confronted the religious foundations of caste. Instead it "constitutionalized" it through caste-based personal laws, failures to reform temple access and to outlaw practices linked to ritual purity. This meant that "the so-called secular state continued to outsource social authority to religion".

If a Dalit chooses to try to escape caste discrimination by converting to religions that in principle are more egalitarian like Christianity or Islam, they are barred by the constitution from accessing reservations. The constitution has effectively trapped Dalits within the Hindu fold, with "no constitutional mechanism to escape the religious identity that legitimizes their oppression".

He concludes that in effect, secularism without caste annihilation only reinforced the very hierarchies it claimed to transcend.

The Fatal Flaw of Impunity for State Officials Who Violate Rights

He also points to a deep, almost fatal flaw of the constitution that while enumerating fundamental rights to secure social justice, it also institutionalises impunity for state functionaries.

Elected public officials, the police, security forces, judges are all protected from disciplinary and criminal action not just when they fail to protect or defend the rights of citizens but even when they violate them. This legal shield protects the state when it fails to uphold rights but also when it directly violates these, while acting with caste, communal and class bias and prejudice.

This impunity renders the marginalized—Dalits, Adivasis, religious minorities, and dissenters—effectively unprotected by India's constitutional order. This means that even custodial torture, rape and killings have no effective redress. For Dalits, Adivasis, and Muslims, he says that this impunity translates into routine terror, incarceration, and erasure. The worst aberration is the power to detain persons without trial or bail, in the way that Teltumbde himself was held.

"The ideals of liberty, equality, and dignity remain distant dreams," he concludes, and these are "betrayed not by enemies of the state but by the state itself".

A democratic republic, Teltumbde affirms luminously, cannot endure on the back of the doctrine of sovereign impunity. It must instead find its strength in the uncompromising pursuit of accountability, especially from those who wield power in its name.

The Way Ahead is Collective Political Assertion

He reflects that perhaps the Constitution could not have been very different from what it is. It was after all a codification of the dominant class's interests into law. "A constitution cannot stand above society", he observes, "it embodies the political will of those who hold power".

For it to genuinely serve the interests of Dalits, it is incumbent upon them to shape their politics in a way that compels the ruling classes to respond. "There can be no messianic solution—only the hard work of collective political assertion".

Prologue

The bond between Dalits and the Indian Constitution is arguably the strongest of all communities in India. Both Dalits and others in society see this deep connection, though from contrasting perspectives. For Dalits, the Constitution carries profound emotional significance, primarily because of its association with Dr. Babasaheb Ambedkar, revered as its chief architect and their liberator. Conversely, many others, shaped by anti-Dalit prejudices, view the Constitution mainly as a document that grants undue privileges to Dalits.

This relationship, however, reveals a paradox. Nowhere have the Constitution's promises faltered more profoundly than in the case of Dalits. While constitutional safeguards and affirmative action have enabled the emergence of a small Dalit middle class, this group remains suspended in a liminal space—excluded from the broader Indian middle class due to the enduring stigma of caste, yet distanced from the Dalit masses with which they share a history but not a present. A visible and vocal minority within this class has even extended its presence internationally, forming a Dalit diaspora that has brought global attention to caste oppression and Ambedkar's legacy. Yet this group represents only the tip of the iceberg—beneath it lies a vast, submerged reality of suffering and despair that continues to define the lives of most Dalits. Ironically, the achievements of this middle class have often obscured the persistent discrimination, exclusion, and exploitation faced by the majority. While their progress is not without significance, it raises a fundamental question: Has the Constitution truly fulfilled its emancipatory promise for Dalits? Regrettably, the answer remains a resounding no.

This book is the final instalment in a ten-volume series that aims to make the Constitution more accessible, especially as we mark its seventy-fifth anniversary. Seventy-five years is a long enough time to ask a simple but important question: Has the Constitution delivered on what it promised? The earlier volumes in this series, written by some of our most respected scholars, generally answer with cautious optimism. They acknowledge that there is a gap between what the Constitution sets out to do and what actually happens on the ground. But most of them place the blame not on the Constitution itself, but on the people responsible for putting it into action. That is a view Ambedkar shared too. He often said that even a great constitution can fail if it is run by the wrong people—and, on the flip side, even a flawed constitution can work well in the hands of good leaders. For him, what really mattered was "constitutional morality"—a term he borrowed from the British historian and political radical George Grote, best known for his *History of Greece*.[1] Ambedkar believed that unless those in power are guided by a deep respect for the values and spirit of the Constitution, no amount of legal text will make a real difference.

Babasaheb Ambedkar saw constitutional morality as something deeper than just following rules—it was about a shared commitment to the spirit of the Constitution. It meant that both those in power and ordinary citizens should act within its framework, not just out of obligation but out of conviction. This kind of moral compass, he believed, was essential for resolving conflicts peacefully, upholding the rule of law, and protecting our basic rights and freedoms. In a country as diverse—and as deeply unequal—as India, nurturing this constitutional morality is not just important; it is absolutely vital. Ambedkar often stressed that the way we govern ourselves must reflect the values built into the Constitution itself. He warned, quite presciently, that if those in charge did not respect this principle, the Constitution—no matter how well written—would be undermined by the very people meant to uphold it. He said:

> "it is perfectly possible to pervert the Constitution, without changing its form by merely changing the form of the administration and to make it inconsistent and opposed to the spirit of the Constitution.[2]

Because the Constitution cannot spell out every administrative detail, Dr. Ambedkar stressed the need for everyone—especially those in power—to cultivate constitutional morality. He famously warned, "Democracy in India is only a top-dressing on an Indian soil, which is essentially undemocratic."[3] In other words, democracy was not something that came naturally to Indian society—it had to be consciously learned, practiced, and nurtured.

Ambedkar did not seem very hopeful that our rulers would rise to this challenge anytime soon. Which leads us to a tough question: Did he also suspect that the Constitution might ultimately fall short of its grand promise? It is hard to say for sure. But when we compare where we are today with the vision laid out in the Preamble, the gap is stark. Liberty is under attack. Economic inequality is worse now than it was even under colonial rule. Fraternity has been shredded by rising communal hatred and growing caste consciousness under the revivalist Hindutva movement. Justice—social, economic, and political—remains elusive. The very foundation of our democracy feels dangerously fragile.

So, what went wrong? It is easy to point fingers at those in power—and to some extent, that blame is justified. But the truth runs deeper. Expecting those driven by power to voluntarily practice constitutional morality may be wishful thinking. If human beings were naturally inclined to do the right thing, we would not need a constitution in the first place. Its whole point is to set up a structure that keeps even the most self-serving leaders in check.

Constitutional morality is not something that just exists

on its own—it has to be cultivated. And that cultivation does not happen in a vacuum. It depends on how seriously we, as a society, engage with the Constitution. To assume that morality will somehow emerge without institutions actively nurturing it is like putting the cart before the horse. It is the Constitution's job not only to set limits, but also to shape the moral habits of those who wield power.

People often say that constitutions are just reflections of society—that they work only as well as the people who operate them. But that view misses something crucial: the power of a constitution to transform society itself. A well-thought-out constitution, one that builds in accountability, checks and balances, and a clear vision of justice, can actually push back against arbitrary power. It can guide those in authority toward more just outcomes. When designed with imagination, a constitution does not just mirror the world—it helps reshape it. It nudges both institutions and social norms in the direction of greater inclusion and equality. So even if it does not set out to spark a revolution, a constitution can still be a powerful tool for social change.

That said, this book does not try to answer all the big philosophical questions about what a constitution can or should do. It sticks to a specific and urgent task: examining what the Indian Constitution has actually done—or failed to do—for Dalits. It is, of course, not shy about pointing out what could have been done and why it was not done.

Any constitution rooted in liberal democratic ideals is

bound to face criticism when judged from the standpoint of the most oppressed. After all, constitutions do not emerge in a vacuum—they codify existing power relations. They often end up institutionalizing the political and economic interests of the dominant classes, all under the respectable cover of legality and democracy. Just look at the last seventy-five years: the patterns of who has thrived and who has suffered under constitutional rule make that much clear.

The book is organized into six chapters. The first two lay the groundwork by explaining the historical and political context behind the special provisions for Dalits in the Constitution. The next three chapters critically examine each of these provisions, exposing how the ruling classes have skilfully manipulated them in the name of social justice. The next chapter shifts focus to broader constitutional features—secular and statist—not directly concerned with Dalits, but disproportionately harming them. The Epilogue ends the discussion by showing how the Constitution created a powerful illusion of Dalit emancipation and transformed Dalits into the most ardent supporters of the constitutional state—despite its persistent failure to liberate them.

The chapters are as follows:

1. Dalits and Nationalist Politics
2. Making of the Indian Constitution
3. Abolition of Untouchability
4. Reservation in Political Representation

5. Reservations in Education and Public Employment
6. Secularism and Issues of Impunity

This book is driven by an unwavering commitment to the belief that the Constitution could—and should—have done far more to realize Dalit aspirations for dignity, equality, and justice. In today's climate, where right-wing reactionary forces openly seek to rewrite or replace the Constitution, such critical engagement with the Constitution runs a risk of being misunderstood as aligning with their agenda. Nothing could be a graver misreading. The book stands firmly on the emancipatory promise of the Preamble—liberty, equality, fraternity, and justice—values the Constitution pledged but has failed to deliver. It unequivocally condemns the right-wing project of resurrecting a mythical past through the imposition of a theocratic, ethnic Hindu Rashtra as a regressive fantasy aimed at entrenching Brahminical supremacy under the guise of national revival. I echo Ambedkar's warning: the establishment of a Hindu Rashtra would be the greatest calamity for India.

Yes, the Constitution is flawed—as the following pages will demonstrate—but dismantling it without first building a genuinely democratic and pro-people alternative would be to destroy the last remaining legal and moral structure within which the struggle for justice can still be waged.

Chapter I

Dalits and Nationalist Politics

"Dalit" is a self-chosen term used by communities once labeled as "Untouchables." These groups have been constitutionally designated as Scheduled Castes (SCs) since 1936. Before 1936, the British called them Depressed Classes, and in some official and missionary documents, they were referred to as Exterior Castes—since they were placed outside the fourfold *varna* system of Hinduism. The term Outcastes was also used to emphasize their exclusion. Some records even called them Panchamas—literally "the fifth *varna*," indicating that they were beyond the fourfold hierarchy. In the south, British administrators popularized the term Pariahs, borrowed from Paraiyar, a large Dalit caste in Tamil Nadu.

Mahatma Gandhi coined the word *Harijan* (meaning "children of God") to refer to these communities. But most Dalits, especially followers of Dr. Ambedkar, rejected it as patronizing. Another term, *Avarna*, meaning "without *varna*," also pointed to their historical exclusion from the caste system.

So where does "Dalit" come from? The word is Sanskrit/ Prakrit in origin, with root "dal" ("to split, crush") as the basis of Marathi Dalit. It first appeared in print as early as 1831 in J. T. Molesworth's *Marathi-English Dictionary* to mean "ground, crushed, reduced to powder".[4] Another dictionary contained the word "Dalita" with meanings "broken, subdued, oppressed."[5]

The modern use of "Dalit" is erroneously attributed to Jotiba Phule (1827–1890), a radical social reformer but it is not true. The word entered political vocabulary in the 1920s through Marathi newspapers and activist circles of Phule's Satya Shodhak Samaj and was often used by Ambedkar in his Marathi speeches and writings in Bahishkru Bharat.[6]The Scheduled Caste Federation (SCF), founded by him in 1942, was popularly called the Dalit Federation in Maharashtra.

How "Dalit" Became a Political and Literary Identity

The SCF's propaganda in Maharashtra, mostly through folk songs in Ambedkari *jalsas*, commonly used the term "Dalit."

In 1958, the Maharashtra Dalit Sahitya Sammelan (literary conference) was organized in Bombay and inaugurated by the communist litterateur Annabhau Sathe[7], where the term "Dalit literature" was used for the first time to describe works authored by Dalits that reflected their lived experiences and struggles.

Inspired by the Black Arts Movement of the 1960s and 1970s in the United States, young Dalit writers in 1970s Maharashtra began expressing their anger and resistance through poetry, fiction, and autobiographies. Since their work did not fit into the sanitized, upper-caste literary conventions, it got its own name: Dalit literature. This movement also gave rise to the Dalit Panthers in 1972, directly influenced by the Black Panther Party in the United States. The Panthers helped popularize the term "Dalit" far beyond Maharashtra, making it a potent symbol of political resistance and cultural assertion. Today, it is an international term. Their ideology also inspired the formation of the Dalit Sangharsh Samiti (DSS) in Karnataka in 1973—a movement that arguably outlasted the Panthers in its influence.

Radical Marathi Dalit writers like Baburao Bagul saw Dalits not just as a caste group but as a revolutionary class, capable of transforming society.[8]

Dalit Demography in India

So how many Dalits are there in India? According to the 2011 Census, about 201.3 million people—or 16.6 percent of the population—were counted as Scheduled Castes. But this figure leaves out Dalit Christians (estimated at 20 million) and Dalit Muslims (roughly 100 million). If these groups were included, the Dalit population would easily exceed 320 million, which is more than 25 percent of India's population. That would make them the third-largest "nation" in the world, population-wise—larger than the combined population of 150 of the least populous countries on the planet.

However, their dispersion across states and districts means Dalits rarely form a numerical majority. A closer look at 2001 Census data shows that in 46 percent of India's districts, Dalits make up 10–19.9 percent of the population; in 25 percent of districts, they comprise 20–49.9 percent. Only 7.4 percent of villages have Dalit majorities, and just 2.6 percent have over 75 percent Dalit population. These are mainly in southern India and often form separate hamlets.[9]

Regionally, Uttar Pradesh, Bihar, West Bengal, and Tamil Nadu together account for nearly half of all Dalits in India. And demographically, Dalits are growing faster than the rest of the population—their share has gone up from 14.8 percent in 1971 to 16.6 percent in 2011, with higher growth rates in rural areas. Despite this, urbanization among Dalits is lower—only 23.74 percent compared to the national urban average of 32.42 percent. Their continued socioeconomic marginalization plays a big role in these trends.

The Complex Social Dynamics among Dalits

It is a misconception to view Dalits as a monolithic group. In reality, Dalit communities have historically mirrored the hierarchical and caste-based discrimination pervasive in the broader caste system, with internal divisions based on subcaste (*jati*) and occupational status. While the Ambedkarite movement significantly weakened these internal hierarchies by promoting solidarity against caste oppression, subcaste consciousness persists, complicating efforts toward complete unity.

- Each state recognizes multiple castes within the Scheduled Castes that maintain strict social boundaries—particularly in matters like marriage and food sharing.[10] Historically, the largest Dalit caste in a given region took the lead in the early Dalit movement.[11] However, after Dr. Ambedkar's rise to prominence—especially following his decisive impact at the Round Table Conferences (1930–32)—he was embraced as their leader.[12] Through this process, as the movement assumed a pan-India character under his leadership, over time minor Dalit castes, influenced by their educated elites, also began seeing Dr. Ambedkar as their leader.[13]
- Yet, since the 1990s, the Rashtriya Swayamsevak Sangh (RSS) has cynically attempted to exploit fractures within Dalit unity by mobilizing minor Dalit castes, amplifying their grievances against dominant Ambedkarite leadership, and reviving alternative caste-specific icons to counter Ambedkar's overarching influence.[14]

Economic and Social Stratification among Dalits

Dalits have always been internally divided—not just by caste labels, but by the kind of work they did and the status that came with it. Take Maharashtra, for instance. Chambhars, who traditionally worked with leather, were generally seen as having a higher status than Mangs, who made ropes. The Mangs, in turn, were considered more skilled than Mahars, who were usually assigned to menial and custodial work. But these rankings were not set in stone.

Things changed depending on where you were and what the economy looked like. In Marathwada, where Mangs were present in larger numbers, many of them became landless labourers—much like the Mahars. But in Vidarbha, where Mangs were fewer and their rope-making or martial skills more in demand, they were relatively better off. These kinds of local and occupational shifts have constantly reshaped the internal hierarchy among Dalit communities over time.[15]

In fact, such changes also meant that groups which did not originally belong to the caste system sometimes got absorbed into Dalit categories. Subcastes merged, broke away, or changed status depending on the social and economic context. There was room—though very constrained—for mobility, both upward and downward.[16]

This unevenness helps explain why some Dalit castes were more likely to take the lead in challenging the caste system. Particularly, those communities that had grown so large in numbers that they could no longer be accommodated in their traditional occupations within a village were forced to look for new ways to live. That search exposed them to new ideas, new people, and new forms of collective struggle. It is no surprise, then, that many of the most important Dalit leaders—including Dr. Ambedkar—came from such castes, like Mahars, who were pushed to the margins but refused to stay there.[17]

Colonial Rule and Dalits

Before the 15th century, no European power had significantly penetrated India. But the global spice trade changed that. The Portuguese, Dutch, Danes, and French came and went—but it was the British East India Company that steadily expanded its hold over the subcontinent.

Initially, British rule was not transformative. Focused on revenue extraction and control, the British leaned on existing social and religious structures, especially Hindu and Islamic legal codes, both steeped in caste. Rather than dismantling caste, they reinforced it—relying on upper-caste landlords for tax collection, thereby deepening caste-based inequalities. As Bernard Cohn notes, the Company's so-called "non-interference" often meant tacit support for dominant castes that helped maintain order.[18]

By the early 19th century, a reformist spirit emerged, shaped by Enlightenment thinkers and pushed by both Indian reformers like Raja Rammohan Roy and Christian missionaries. Under Governor-General William Bentinck, practices like *sati*, *thuggee*, and female infanticide were abolished. Bentinck outlawed *sati* in 1829, justifying it through utilitarian moral reasoning.[19] Reforms such as the

Hindu Widows' Remarriage Act of 1856 were framed as moral progress but also served colonial interests: bolstering British legitimacy among reformist elites and missionary lobbies.[20]

These intrusions into religious and social customs, however, provoked backlash. Replacing Persian and Sanskrit with English, introducing missionaries, and mixing castes in the army—especially deploying Dalits alongside high castes—violated ritual boundaries. The infamous greased-cartridge episode symbolized these transgressions. These disruptions culminated in the 1857 revolt, which united disaffected elites. After the revolt, the British crown took direct control of India. Queen Victoria issued 1858 Proclamation that promised non-interference in religious and social customs.

The colonial state overtly concerned to control India, went on measuring every possible thing of her with a dictum, "you cannot control what you do not measure." They adopted national census from 1871 and began counting caste from 1881. The British sought to fit India's countless jatis into the Brahminical fourfold varna system, distorting their relational local identities. As Arjun Appadurai argues, this classificatory impulse didn't just describe caste—it *produced* it as a rigid, bureaucratized identity.[21] The census also fostered competition among castes for higher rank, solidifying boundaries that were previously contextual and fluid.

Legal codification reinforced this. The Indian Penal Code (1860) and the Indian Evidence Act (1872) enshrined caste-based personal laws into colonial jurisprudence.[22] Caste also reshaped the military. After 1857, the British excluded Brahmins and Muslims from rebel regions and privileged "martial races" like Sikhs and Gurkhas—while categorizing Dalits as non-martial, effectively barring their recruitment.[23]

By the late 19th century, Dalits were officially labelled "Depressed Classes." Ethnographers like Herbert Risley promoted racial theories linking caste to physical attributes, feeding into colonial governance. As Nicholas Dirks notes, caste became central to statecraft—reimagined from a local social code into a tool of colonial rule.[24]

This recognition was a double-edged sword. It gave visibility to oppressed groups but also hardened caste lines, locking identities into state-administered categories—a logic that the postcolonial state would inherit through the constitutional recognition of Scheduled Castes.

Thus, British rule did not create caste, as some Hindutva propagandists insinuate[25], but it decisively transformed it—fixing what was once a dynamic, localized system into a rigid, institutionalized hierarchy. This colonial legacy continues to reverberate in India's social and political life.

Caste and the Politics of "Divide and Rule"

The British strategy of "divide and rule" took formal shape with the Indian Councils Act of 1909 (Morley-Minto Reforms), which introduced separate electorates for Muslims, institutionalizing religious identity in politics and fragmenting the nascent nationalist movement. During these deliberations, a delegation led by Aga Khan suggested that Untouchables and Adivasis be categorized separately from Hindus—an idea reflected in the 1911 Census through the trifurcation of Hindus into "Hindus," "Depressed Classes," and "Animists."

Colonial caste policy did not merely reflect difference—it produced and institutionalized it, laying the foundation for enduring caste-based political alignments.[26]

An Unintended Empowerment of Dalits

Despite the reification of caste, British rule inadvertently created new avenues for Dalits—through military recruitment, administrative roles, and education. Communities like the Mahars, Namasudras, and Parayars saw significant presence in the British Indian Army, particularly before 1857. The Mahars, for instance, constituted one-sixth of Bombay Presidency's regiments, with a strong presence of non-commissioned officers.[27]

Barred from elite military positions in Hindu kingdoms, Dalits were unencumbered by the taboos that restricted upper castes. Post-1857, the British distrusted high-caste sepoys and favoured recruits seen as socially marginal but politically loyal.[28] Dalits also performed stigmatized but vital tasks—handling corpses, sanitation, and logistics—gaining access to stable incomes, cantonment schools, and urban life.[29]

Such roles extended beyond the military. Dalits

employed in British clubs, railways, and administrative offices were exposed to English education and less rigid caste hierarchies. Many Dalit leaders—Ambedkar, M. C. Rajah, and Swami Achhutanand—came from families connected to these colonial institutions.[30] In his 1936 Mahad speech, Ambedkar noted how Mahar women, through military life, gained literacy and confidence to interpret religious texts publicly—a radical shift for Dalit women.[31]

Although the British had no intention of dismantling caste, their pragmatism opened spaces where Dalits accessed modern education, employment, and political awareness—cracks through which future movements emerged.

Religious and Social Mobilization

Christian missionaries, predating British rule, were among the earliest to provide Dalits access to education and dignity. Mahatma Phule, educated in a missionary school, exemplifies how these institutions underpinned early anti-caste reform. By the late 19th century, Dalits were also drawn to cities due to colonial infrastructure projects—railways, ports, and factories—gaining economic mobility and forming the nucleus of modern Dalit political assertion.

Dalit religious movements emerged across India—often in direct challenge to Brahminism. Harichand Thakur's Matua sect (East Bengal, 1860) and Phule's Sarvajanik Satya Dharma (1873) are early examples. Their strategies included:

- Claiming higher ritual status (e.g., Kshatriya ancestry);
- Dissociating from Hindu identity (e.g., Iyothee Thass's assertion of Buddhist origin);
- Demanding state support for socioeconomic upliftment.

Movements like Adi Dharm (Punjab), Adi Hindu (U.P.), Adi Andhra, Adi Karnataka, and Adi Dravida in South India challenged caste hierarchies by reclaiming alternative genealogies and asserting indigenous status.[32]

Activism took multiple forms—community meetings, journals, pamphlets, hostels, and libraries. Ayyankali, an illiterate Pulayar youth from Travancore, led a more confrontational struggle through physical assertion of Dalit rights.[33] Still, it was with Ambedkar that Dalit assertion found its most coherent, national articulation.

Congress Attitude toward Dalits

The Indian National Congress, established in 1885, was dominated by English-educated elites, landlords, and emerging capitalists who prioritized political reforms over social change. To maintain nationalist unity, it steered clear of contentious social issues like caste, untouchability, and women's rights, viewing them as distractions from the goal of self-rule.

A parallel movement, the Social Conference, led by reformers like M. G. Ranade and G. K. Gokhale, emphasized social reform. However, these efforts were constrained by upper-caste sensibilities and focused more on moderate reforms such as widow remarriage, child marriage, and the abolition of untouchability. Radical transformations, such as those envisioned by Jotiba Phule or later by Babasaheb Ambedkar, were beyond its scope. By 1895, after Congress refused to incorporate social reform into its agenda at the Pune session, the Social Conference began meeting separately and gradually declined in influence.

While the 1895 Swaraj Constitution—drafted by nationalists like Bal Gangadhar Tilak—proposed civil liberties and equality before law, it omitted any specific safeguards for Dalits. It marked a nominal commitment to equality but avoided addressing caste oppression directly.[34] Congress's reluctance to confront caste remained unchanged until the 1917 Calcutta session under Annie Besant, where it passed a resolution urging removal of untouchability—its first official acknowledgment, though devoid of concrete measures.

Mahatma Gandhi brought untouchability to the fore from 1916 onward, calling Dalits "Harijans" and championing temple entry and access to public spaces. The Congress's 1920 Nagpur session reiterated this moral commitment. However, Gandhi's approach framed untouchability as a social sin to be atoned for by caste Hindus rather than a systemic injustice needing political redress.

The 1928 Nehru Report—a response to the Simon Commission—advocated civil rights and access to public institutions but avoided political safeguards like reservations. It aligned with Gandhi's view of untouchability as a moral issue, resisting Ambedkar's demands for separate electorates and structural empowerment.

The Congress's progressive Karachi Resolution of 1931 called for fundamental rights and the abolition of untouchability, but the core Gandhi-Ambedkar rift continued. The 1932 Poona Pact, a compromise forced upon Ambedkar, secured reserved seats for Dalits within the general electorate. Gandhi subsequently formed the Harijan Sevak Sangh, focusing on uplift through social work rather than political empowerment.

In the late 1930s, Congress-led provincial governments undertook modest efforts to improve Dalit education and employment and supported temple entry movements such as the Vaikom (1924–25) and Guruvayur (1931–32) agitations. Yet these initiatives were often hindered by internal conservative opposition.

By 1946, facing growing Dalit mobilization and the necessity of political accommodation, Congress acknowledged the need for reservations in education, employment, and legislatures. Still, its historical trajectory reveals a consistent pattern: from neglect to moral sympathy, without embracing Ambedkar's transformative agenda. Congress's support for Dalits was shaped more by political pragmatism than by a structural commitment to annihilating caste.

Ambedkar and the Colonial Constitution

Armed with formidable academic credentials, Dr. Ambedkar shifted the Dalit movement from internal reform to civil rights and political advocacy, as colonial politics opened along communal lines following the Morley-Minto Reforms of 1909 (referred to before), which introduced separate electorates for Muslims[35] and seeded the idea of separation of Dalits and Adivasis from caste Hindus.

Initially, Ambedkar believed that Dalit assertion would push progressive caste Hindus toward reform. However, the violent backlash to the 1927 Mahad Satyagraha[36]—when caste Hindus denied Dalits access to the Chowdar tank and secured a court injunction—shattered this belief.[37] Disillusioned, Ambedkar turned to political action, articulating Dalits as a distinct political entity and calling for religious conversion as a path out of Hindu identity.[38]

Unlike Indian nationalists who boycotted the Simon Commission (1928) due to its all-European composition, Dalit leaders engaged with it, seeing it as neutral. They submitted memoranda demanding reserved seats, executive representation, public service quotas, and universal franchise.[39] The Commission's 1930 report acknowledged Dalit grievances and proposed reserved seats within joint electorates, with gubernatorial certification of Dalit candidates to protect representation. Ambedkar rejected this as inadequate, insisting on separate electorates.[40]

At the 1930 Nagpur Depressed Classes Conference,

Ambedkar criticized British use of Dalit suffering to justify delaying Indian self-rule.[41] In response, Dalit organizations unified to demand communal electorates, leading to Ambedkar and Rettamalai Srinivasan's invitation to the Round Table Conferences in London.

At the First Round Table Conference (1930), Dr Ambedkar demanded that the Depressed Classes be recognized as a minority entitled to separate representation, including reserved seats, legal protections, cabinet inclusion, and safeguards against discrimination.[42] The Minorities Sub-Committee acknowledged these concerns, noting the risks of marginalization under joint electorates.[43]

In the Second Round Table Conference (1931), Ambedkar clashed with Gandhi, who opposed separate electorates for Dalits and framed untouchability as a social problem to be solved within Hindu society. Ambedkar, however, maintained that only political safeguards—particularly separate electorates—could ensure real representation. He suggested alternative designations like "Non-Caste Hindus" or "Protestant Hindus" to mark Dalit political autonomy.[44]

Despite Gandhi's opposition, the 1932 Communal Award issued by British Prime Minister Ramsay MacDonald granted Dalits separate electorates and double voting rights—one within separate Dalit constituencies and another in the general electorate—reserving 71 out of 1,508 provincial legislature seats.[45]

Gandhi, fearing this would fracture Hindu unity and empower Muslim League claims to parity, launched a fast unto death while imprisoned in Yerwada Jail.[46] Legal experts, including Sir Tej Bahadur Sapru, brokered a compromise—the Poona Pact—which replaced separate electorates with:

- Joint electorates and an enhanced quantum of reserved seats for Dalits;
- Reservation in the central assembly;
- A two-stage election: Dalits would shortlist candidates, and the general electorate would vote;
- Dalit-nominated candidates in certain seats.[47]

Ambedkar and M. C. Rajah accepted this with modifications—148 reserved seats in provincial legislatures and 18 percent of central legislature seats—proportional to the Dalit population among Hindus. The duration of the arrangement was left open to review, while Congress pledged support for Dalit welfare through education, employment, and economic initiatives.[48]

These terms were institutionalized in the Government of India Act, 1935, which formally recognized "Scheduled Castes" (Section 24, Schedule I) and initiated caste enumeration to operationalize reserved representation.[49]

Chapter II

Making of the Indian Constitution

In 1942, amid World War II, the British government sent Sir Stafford Cripps to India with a proposal for self-government. It envisioned an elected Constituent Assembly, formed through proportional representation by provincial legislatures, which would draft a constitution and sign a treaty with the British Crown. The proposal guaranteed safeguards for racial and religious minorities and left India free to determine its relationship with the Commonwealth.

Babasaheb Ambedkar opposed the plan, noting its failure to ensure political safeguards for the Depressed Classes, unlike the Government of India Act, 1935. He feared the Assembly would be dominated by caste Hindus and that proportional representation—"Members of this body shall be elected by the members of the Lower Houses of the Provincial Legislatures, and the representation of each community shall be in proportion to its population"—would marginalize Dalits.

The Indian National Congress also rejected the Cripps proposals on April 2, 1942, citing their vagueness and British control over defence. In response to the deadlock, the Quit India Movement was launched on August 8, demanding complete British withdrawal. Congress also proposed forming a provisional government and drafting its own constitution.

In the aftermath, Ambedkar's SCF passed a resolution on September 23, 1944, demanding:

- Recognition of Scheduled Castes as a distinct political category;
- Earmarked funds for education;
- Separate settlements on reserved land;
- Adequate representation in legislatures, public services, and commissions;
- Fundamental Rights immune to legislative amendments;
- An independent authority (akin to the Auditor General) to enforce safeguards.

To address these tensions, the Sapru Committee (1945) proposed a 143-member assembly with 51 seats for caste Hindus, 51 for Muslims, 20 for Scheduled Castes, and the rest for Sikhs, Christians, and tribal groups.

Ambedkar remained skeptical. He argued that an assembly elected by a Hindu-majority electorate would deny Dalits genuine representation. Without separate electorates and constitutional safeguards, their rights would be subordinated to caste Hindu dominance. He told the Federation that a new assembly was unnecessary; the 1935 Act was adequate.[50]

World War II ended with Germany's surrender on May 8 and Japan's on September 2, 1945. Britain, weakened and unable to suppress unrest—fuelled by the INA trials and the 1946 Royal Indian Navy Mutiny—sent the Cabinet Mission (Pethick-Lawrence, Stafford Cripps, and A. V. Alexander) to negotiate India's transition. On May 16, 1946, the Cabinet Mission Plan proposed a Constituent Assembly, indirectly elected by provincial assemblies formed via the January 1946 elections. The SCF, having won only two seats, had no realistic hope of entering the Constituent Assembly (CA).

The CA, constituted in May 1946, was not directly elected. Voting rights for provincial assemblies were restricted by property, tax, and education qualifications; only 28.5 percent of adults were eligible.[51] After Partition, its strength fell to 299, including 70 princely-state nominees. Effective popular representation dropped to around 20 percent. The Congress party had an overwhelming majority. Austin observed: "The Assembly, the Congress, and the government were...like the points of a triangle...assuming a form infinitely meaningful for India[52]."

Of the twenty most influential members of the CA, all were university graduates; four studied abroad (Nehru, Patel, Ambedkar, and Azad). Twelve were lawyers; others included a doctor, teachers, civil servants, and a businessman. Religiously, the Assembly had two Muslims, one Christian, and the rest Hindus—including Ambedkar as the only Dalit, nine Brahmins, and seven from other upper castes. Fifteen had strong Congress ties; five, including Ambedkar and Saadulla (Muslim League), were independent or opponents.[53]

In class terms, the CA thus was dominated by upper-caste, Western-educated elites, landlords, and capitalists, with limited participation from workers, peasants, or marginalized groups. This elite makeup shaped a constitution aimed more at continuity than radical transformation. The Congress, aligned with capitalist and landlord interests, preserved their dominance under the guise of nationalist and anticolonial rhetoric.

Post-independence, the colonial state structure remained largely intact, not by default but by design. Michael Brecher noted that 250 of the Constitution's 395 articles were directly derived from the 1935 Act.[54] Industrialist G. D. Birla candidly admitted: "We have embodied large portions of the [1935] Act in the Constitution... which shows that in it was cast the pattern of our future plans."[55] Ambedkar himself acknowledged that "the Draft Constitution has produced a good part of the provisions of the Government of India Act, 1935" and justified it saying, "I make no apologies. There is nothing to be ashamed of in borrowing. It involves no plagiarism. Nobody holds any patent rights in the fundamental ideas of a Constitution."[56]

Ambedkar was elected to the Assembly from the Jessore-Khulna constituency in Bengal on July 19, 1946, despite strong Congress opposition. However, the Mountbatten Plan of June 3, 1947, placed his seat in Pakistan. He was subsequently re-elected from Bombay Province through Congress support from Pune.[57]

Initial Draft Constitution by B. N. Rau

To facilitate the drafting process, the CA appointed Benegal Narsing Rau, a senior civil servant and jurist, as constitutional advisor. Rau, assisted by Dr. Surendra Nath Mukerjee, joint secretary and draftsman, began work in September 1947 and submitted a comprehensive initial draft in October 1947. This draft—based on reports from twenty-two committees and influenced by the constitutions of the United States, United Kingdom, Australia, Canada, and Ireland—contained 240 clauses and thirteen schedules.

Provisions for SCs and STs in Rau's Draft

- Legislative reservations: Reserved seats for SCs under a joint electorate system, in line with the Poona Pact (1932).
- Public employment: Advocated SC inclusion in government jobs, albeit without a robust framework.
- Untouchability: Implicit legal opposition to caste discrimination, which later became Article 17.
- Socioeconomic safeguards: Recommended state-supported education, land redistribution, and employment for SCs.

- Scheduled Tribes: Provided a distinct classification with added emphasis on administrative autonomy, laying the basis for
  - Fifth Schedule (mainland tribal areas);
  - Sixth Schedule (Northeastern tribal areas).

Drafting Committee and Review

On August 29, 1947, the CA formed a Drafting Committee comprising Alladi Krishnaswami Ayyar, N. Gopalaswami Ayyangar, Dr. B. R. Ambedkar (chairman), K. M. Munshi, Mohammad Saadulla, B. L. Mitter, and D. P. Khaitan, to revise Rau's draft.

Major Revisions by the Drafting Committee

1. Expanded Preamble: Replaced Rau's minimalist preamble with a detailed declaration defining India as a Sovereign Democratic Republic (later amended in 1976 to include "Socialist" and "Secular").
2. Strengthened Fundamental Rights:
   - Article 32 (Right to Constitutional Remedies), called the "heart and soul" of the Constitution by Ambedkar.
   - Article 17 (Abolition of Untouchability), made explicit.
   - Articles 23–24, banning forced labor (*begar*) and child labor.

3. Affirmative Action and Tribal Autonomy:
    - Articles 330, 332, 335, and 16(4) strengthened SC/ST representation in legislatures and jobs.
    - Fifth and Sixth Schedules institutionalized tribal self-governance.
4. Directive Principles (Part IV):
    - Articulated state duties on social and economic justice.
    - Article 39 emphasized equitable distribution of wealth and resources.
5. Shift to Parliamentary System:
    - Rejected Rau's U.S.-style presidential model in favor of the British Westminster system.
6. Citizenship (Articles 5–11):
    - Introduced clear provisions, especially for Partition-era refugees.
7. Amendment Process (Article 368):
    - Replaced Rau's rigid process with a more flexible mechanism.
8. Fundamental Rights vs. Directive Principles:
    - Made Fundamental Rights enforceable; Directive Principles nonjusticiable but directive in governance.
9. Language Policy (Articles 343–351):
    - Declared Hindi the official language (with English for fifteen years); protected linguistic minorities.

10. Emergency Provisions (Articles 352–360):
    - The Drafting Committee also introduced powers for National, State, and Financial Emergencies, absent in Rau's draft.

Limitations on Fundamental Rights

Rau's draft, influenced by the U.S. Constitution, granted broad, unrestricted rights. However, at the behest of Nehru and Patel, the Drafting Committee introduced "reasonable restrictions" to balance individual liberty with public order and national interest.

Key modifications included:

1. Right to Equality (Articles 14–18):
    - Article 15(4): Enabled special provisions for SCs, STs, and SEBCs.
    - Article 16(4): Allowed job reservations for backward classes.
2. Right to Freedom (Article 19):
    - Introduced restrictions on speech, assembly, association, movement, and occupation for reasons such as public order, morality, national security, and sovereignty (later elaborated in the First Amendment, 1951).
3. Article 21: Replaced "due process" with "procedure established by law" to limit judicial activism.
4. Article 22: Allowed preventive detention up to three months for national security.

5. Religious Freedom (Articles 25–28):
   - Article 25(1): Subjected to public health, morality, order, and social reform.
   - Article 28: Banned religious instruction in state-funded schools; permitted in private/minority institutions.
6. Right to Property (Article 31):
   - Initially a fundamental right with compensation; downgraded to a legal right by the Forty-fourth Amendment (1978).

Finalization of the Draft Constitution

Between October 1947 and February 1948, the Drafting Committee revised B. N. Rau's original draft, culminating in the publication of the Draft Constitution on February 21, 1948. It comprised 315 articles across 18 parts and 8 schedules. Crucially, it introduced explicit safeguards for Scheduled Castes (SCs) and Scheduled Tribes (STs), including:

- Legislative reservations (Articles 330, 332);
- Public employment reservations (Article 335 and Article 16(4));
- Enhanced autonomy for tribal areas through expanded Fifth and Sixth Schedules.

The draft was debated in the Constituent Assembly from October 1947 to February 1949. After an eight-month public review, a second draft was prepared in October 1948. Final debates were held from November to October 1949, leading to the adoption of the Constitution on November 26, 1949.

Debates on Safeguards for Dalits

One of the most contentious issues during constitution making was ensuring justice for Dalits. While most Assembly members agreed on the need for uplift of SCs, opinions varied on how best to achieve it. Some viewed reservations as incompatible with liberal democratic ideals; others insisted that legal equality without structural interventions would be insufficient to dismantle entrenched caste hierarchies.

The Minorities Sub-Committee recommended a pragmatic approach: targeted development and antidiscrimination measures. Political reservations for SCs and STs were accepted, albeit for a limited duration of ten years—since extended repeatedly. The Constitution also made provisions for Backward Classes—primarily the lower Shudra castes—mandating a commission to identify and recommend measures for their advancement.

Concerns were raised about the potential misuse of caste-based reservations and the risk of further social fragmentation. Yet there was broad consensus on some foundational issues: the CA unanimously declared untouchability a punishable offense. Still, some members rightly questioned how untouchability could be eradicated without addressing the root problem—caste itself. Others warned that without clear legal definitions and mechanisms, these provisions might lack force.

Ultimately, the Constitution enshrined a range of political, social, and economic safeguards for Dalits—tools intended to secure a more equitable future. But their efficacy remains in question. Despite constitutional guarantees, the lived reality for many Dalits is still defined by marginalization. While a section has achieved upward mobility, the broader community continues to struggle. This raises a pressing question: Have constitutional promises translated into meaningful change?

Chapter III

Abolition of Untouchability

The abolition of untouchability is often hailed as one of the CA's most radical achievements. This chapter offers a critical assessment of this decision in the light of empirical evidence of its failure and probes the reasons therefor.

For centuries, Dalits endured a unique and brutal regime of exclusion, humiliation, and dehumanization under the caste order—an experience with few parallels in the world. During colonial rule, privileged caste elites who came into contact with the West began to experience embarrassment over this inhuman practice, prompting some to denounce it. But it was the growing political assertion of Dalits, fuelled by a rising consciousness of their degraded condition, that gave urgency to the issue. As Dalits staked claim to a distinct political identity, it threatened to disturb the fragile equation between the Congress and the Muslim League. What began as a paternalistic reform project driven by a few upper-caste voices, particularly Mahatma Gandhi's moral campaign, soon became a rhetorical centerpiece of Congress politics—more symbolic than substantive.

Babasaheb Ambedkar, however, was very clear: he had spoken about "annihilation of caste" more than a decade earlier. But now the circumstances were different: he was a member of the Congress Assembly Party and the chairman of the Drafting Committee of the Constituent Assembly.

B. N. Rau's draft of the Constitution had spoken against discrimination but did not explicitly mention untouchability. The Drafting Committee, in its review of the draft, inserted a specific article criminalizing the practice of untouchability. When the revised draft of the Constitution came up for debate—ironically piloted by Ambedkar in the Constituent Assembly—some members expressed reservations, echoing his previous view about annihilation of caste. The irony was that he was silent in the debate.

Pramatha Ranjan Thakur, great-grandson of Harichand Thakur, the founder of the Matua sect (the first Dalit reform movement) and the first barrister from the Namasudra community in Bengal, for instance, argued: "I do not understand how you can abolish untouchability without abolishing the very caste system. Untouchability is nothing but the symptom of the disease, namely, the caste system... Unless we can do away with the caste system altogether there is no use tinkering with the problem of untouchability superficially."[58] Thakur would remain the lone SC member who critiqued the conceptually faulty proposal.

Another member, Suresh Chandra Banerjee, a distinguished scholar of ancient Indian history and literature, also endorsed Thakur's view, saying, "Untouchability is merely a symptom, the root cause is caste distinction and unless and until the root cause is removed, untouchability in some form or other is bound to exist."[59] Still another member, D. N. Datta, who would contribute to Pakistan's Constituent Assembly after Partition, and who was another member from Bengal endorsing this view, emphatically said: "...the root cause of untouchability, namely, the caste system, in Hindu society should be abolished altogether. Unless the caste system is abolished, untouchability will persist in some form or other.... unless Hindu society is drastically reformed by abolishing the caste system, it [Hindu society] is bound to perish. Caste system should be abolished."[60] Both these gentlemen belonged to privileged castes and upper-class backgrounds—Banerjee being a Brahmin and Dhirendranath Datta from an aristocratic Kayastha family of Ramrail in Brahmanbaria district (now in Bangladesh).

These were consequential interventions, yet they were ignored amid the euphoria of the Constituent Assembly over abolition of untouchability. Interestingly, none of the other Scheduled Caste members raised any such objection or even spoke in support of these arguments. Why? Perhaps they feared that the abolition of caste would jeopardize reservations. But why did the CA itself not take caste abolition seriously? Was caste truly unabolishable? We may ponder these questions a while later.

So, on November 29, 1947, the Constituent Assembly unanimously passed the resolution to abolish untouchability and criminalize its practice. Article 17 (in the final Constitution) thus was born. It stated: "Untouchability is abolished and its practice in any form is forbidden. The enforcement of any disability arising out of untouchability shall be an offence punishable in accordance with law." Many members spoke jubilantly about it. Hansa Mehta, while generally opposed to granting any rights to minorities beyond what the Constitution provided, made a notable exception for the Scheduled Castes. She strongly supported the abolition of untouchability, calling it "the greatest thing that we have done," a move that "posterity will be very, very proud of."[61] Many endorsed it and shared their perspectives. Ajit Prasad Jain described untouchability as "essentially an economic disease[62]," while V. I. Muniswamy Pillai, himself a Scheduled Caste member from Madras, welcomed the constitutional provision but demanded special laws to ensure its enforcement.[63] Naziruddin Ahmad, a prominent voice from the Muslim League within the Constituent Assembly from Bengal, raised concerns over the lack of definition, suggesting that untouchability be explicitly tied to religion and caste.[64] Mono Mohan Das, another SC member from Bengal, hailed November 29, 1948, as "a great and memorable day for us, the untouchables[65]." Dakshayani Velayudhan, the youngest and only Scheduled Caste woman in the Assembly from Kerala, echoed this sentiment, noting that "our delegates abroad will not have to hang their heads in shame if somebody raises such a question in an organisation of international nature," betraying her party's (Congress's) concern.[66] Her speeches emphasized that the success of constitutional safeguards depended not only on legal provisions but also on societal attitudes and collective action.[67] K. T. Shah, an economist and socialist, extended Naziruddin Ahmad's concern about the lack of clarity and remarked that the "Constitution lacks very much in a definition clause[68]," highlighting that untouchability could manifest in various forms beyond religion and caste. Despite such concerns, the general mood in the Assembly was one of euphoria and pride over the decision to constitutionally abolish untouchability.

On that day none—except the three Bengali gentlemen cited above—raised a whisper of doubt as to how untouchability could be abolished when the castes were left untouched.

Empirical Evidence of the Failure

After seven decades of the working of the Constitution, untouchability continues to be the bane of Dalit lives. Several surveys since the 1960s have revealed that constitutional provisions have had little impact on eliminating untouchability in villages across India. Key studies include:

- All India Survey on Untouchability (1965) by N. S. Jodha

- A. R. Desai's study on rural sociology (1969)
- G. S. Ghurye's *Caste and Race in India* (1969)
- Kaka Kalelkar Committee Report (1955, cited in subsequent studies)
- G. Shah's Gujarat survey on untouchability (1970s)
- Iqbal Narain and P. C. Mathur study (1976)—Rajasthan
- S. C. Dube's study on village India (1977)
- Sukhadeo Thorat's studies (1980s–1990s)
- National Sample Survey Office (NSSO) reports (1983–2000)
- Mandal Commission Report (1980)
- Bihar Harijan Inquiry Committee Report (1980s)
- Andhra Pradesh Commission on SC/ST Welfare (1980s–1990s)
- Reports of the National Commission for Scheduled Castes, 2018–19 and 2019–20

We may just consider three recent studies conducted in the twenty-first century to see the present state of untouchability.

1. ActionAid Survey (2001–2)

The ActionAid survey conducted between 2001 and 2002 offers a grim snapshot of how untouchability continues to shape life in rural India. Covering 565 villages across eleven major states, the survey lays bare how deeply caste-based discrimination remains woven into everyday experience for Dalit communities.

One of the clearest signs of this exclusion is where people live. Dalit settlements are usually set apart from those of dominant castes, physically reinforcing caste hierarchies and cutting Dalits off from basic services and shared community spaces. This separation spills over into routine interactions in public life. In nearly half the villages surveyed—48.2 percent—Dalits are still denied access to common water sources.

Even schools, which are supposed to foster equality, are not free from this prejudice. Around 38 percent of government schools were found to make Dalit children sit separately during mid-day meals. In health care too, caste bias takes its toll—health workers in one-third of the villages surveyed reportedly refused to visit Dalit homes.

Religious and social exclusion is just as widespread. In 64 percent of the villages, Dalits were barred from entering temples. In 73 percent, they were not allowed into non-Dalit homes, and in 70 percent, they could not share meals with non-Dalits. These are not just occasional slights—they are daily reminders of entrenched inequality.

The economic sphere offers little relief. In many areas, Dalits are not allowed to sell goods like milk or even access basic services from traditional caste-based occupations like barbers and washermen. Shockingly, in 36 percent of the villages, Dalits could not even enter local shops—cutting them off from economic participation altogether.

Even political representation—guaranteed by law—falls

short in practice. In many panchayats, Dalit members are systematically excluded from decision-making, rendering their positions symbolic rather than meaningful.

What the ActionAid survey reveals is not a scattered set of problems but a consistent and systemic pattern of caste-based discrimination. It affects every aspect of Dalit life—where they live, what they eat, how they learn, how they earn, and even how they worship. These findings serve as a stark reminder that untouchability is far from abolished in practice. It remains a powerful tool of social control, continuing to deny Dalits the dignity and equality that the Constitution so clearly promises.

2. Navsarjan Survey in Gujarat (2010)

The 2010 *Understanding Untouchability* study, conducted by the Navsarjan Trust and the Robert F. Kennedy Center for Justice and Human Rights, offers a comprehensive examination of caste-based discrimination in Gujarat. Surveying 1,589 villages with 5,462 respondents, the study uncovered widespread and systemic practices of untouchability affecting Dalits in both public and private spheres. The study sought responses on ninety-eight forms of untouchability and found that:

- 98.1 percent of villages did not allow Dalits to rent houses in non-Dalit neighborhoods.
- 90.8 percent of villages barred Dalits from temples.

- 98 percent of non-Dalits maintained separate utensils for Dalits.
- 73 percent of villages denied Dalits access to barbers.
- 61 percent of villages restricted Dalit use of potters' services.
- 29 percent of villages denied Dalits access to drinking water.

Some key findings noted in their report[69] are:

- Segregation in public facilities: Dalits faced exclusion from common resources, including segregated housing, separate drinking water wells, and restricted access to places of worship. In many instances, Dalits were denied entry to temples and faced barriers in accessing public wells, leading to reliance on separate, and often inferior, facilities.[70]
- Discrimination in education: The study highlighted discriminatory practices in schools, such as separate seating arrangements and utensils for Dalit students during mid-day meals. This segregation fostered an environment of exclusion and adversely impacted the educational experiences of Dalit children.[71]
- Social exclusion and economic marginalization: Dalits were often barred from participating in community events and faced discrimination in employment opportunities. Traditional caste-based occupations were enforced, limiting economic

mobility and perpetuating cycles of poverty within Dalit communities.

- Intra-Dalit discrimination: The research uncovered "horizontal" discrimination, where subcastes within the Dalit community practiced untouchability against each other. This internal stratification further fragmented the community and exacerbated social inequalities.
- Non-implementation of protective laws: Despite the existence of legal frameworks like the Scheduled Castes and the Scheduled Tribes (Prevention of Atrocities) Act, 1989, enforcement was found to be lacking. The persistence of discriminatory practices indicated a significant gap between legislation and ground realities.

This extensive study underscores the entrenched nature of caste-based discrimination in Gujarat, revealing that despite constitutional safeguards, untouchability remains pervasive.

3. India Human Development Survey (IHDS-2), 2011–12

The India Human Development Survey (IHDS) of 2011–12, conducted jointly by the National Council of Applied Economic Research (NCAER) and the University of Maryland, offers a sobering look at the continued persistence of untouchability. It showed that untouchability remains an entrenched reality, woven into the fabric of everyday life. Key findings were:

- Enduring social segregation: Dalits continue to face exclusion in education, employment, and religious participation.
- Institutional discrimination: Even state institutions, including schools and health-care services, exhibit caste-based bias.
- Intersection of caste, class, and gender: Dalit women face compounded discrimination, including systemic violence.
- Resilience of caste ideology: The persistence of untouchability underscores the deep-seated entrenchment of caste hierarchy in Indian society.
- National average: Approximately 27 percent of Indian households admitted to practicing untouchability.[72]
- Rural vs. urban: The practice is more prevalent in rural areas (30 percent) compared to urban settings (20 percent).[73]

Caste and Religious Dynamics

- Brahmins: 52 percent acknowledged practicing untouchability.
- Other Backward Classes (OBCs): 33 percent admitted to the practice.
- Non-Brahmin forward castes: 24 percent reported engaging in untouchability.
- Scheduled Castes (SCs): 11 percent admitted to practicing untouchability, indicating internalized caste-based discrimination.

- Scheduled Tribes (STs): 17 percent reported practicing untouchability.
- Religious communities: Other than Hindus, the practice was reported among Sikhs (23 percent), Muslims (18 percent), and Christians (5 percent), highlighting its prevalence beyond Hindu communities.[74]

Regional Variations

- Higher prevalence: Central Plains (49 percent), Northern (40 percent), and Hilly regions (38 percent).
- Lower prevalence: Southern, Eastern, and Western regions (the findings of the Navsarjan survey of Gujarat, as seen above, contradict this) exhibited lower instances of the practice.[75]

Influence of Education and Income

- Education: Households with higher educational attainment showed a reduced tendency to practice untouchability. Notably, among Brahmins and OBCs, there was a significant decline in the practice as education levels increased.
- Income: Wealthier households were less likely to engage in untouchability practices. The incidence decreased from 33 percent among the poorest to 23 percent among the richest households.[76]

Social Networks

Surprisingly, households with broader social ties beyond caste were more likely to practice untouchability—highlighting that casual interaction does little to challenge entrenched prejudice. This points to the structural, cross-cutting nature of untouchability across class and region. While its decline may suggest progress, crediting constitutional safeguards alone overstates their role. In truth, the erosion of overt practices like touch-me-notism stems more from capitalist expansion—through public transport, markets—and sustained Dalit resistance that demanded access to public spaces. Yet the caste consciousness underpinning untouchability persists, reinforced by its continued recognition in the constitutional and administrative framework.

Anecdotal Evidence of Untouchability

Beyond statistics, a grim pattern of journalistic and anecdotal evidence across India reveals that caste remains a violent, oppressive social code. Untouchability is not a relic—it is a living reality enforced through routine humiliation, assault, and murder.

Across states, Dalits have faced brutal attacks for acts seen as "caste transgressions." In Tamil Nadu (2015), a youth was killed for riding a horse at his wedding. In Madhya Pradesh (2021), a Dalit groom wore a helmet to shield himself from stones. In Bulandshahr (2025), upper-caste men dragged a groom off his horse, beat guests, and hurled caste slurs. These are merely a few random instances drawn from a gruesome, recurring pattern of atrocities reported every year. In 2025 alone, Citizens for Justice and Peace (CJP) formally lodged a complaint with the National Commission for Scheduled Castes (NCSC), documenting thirty anti-Dalit atrocities across several states—including Uttar Pradesh, Madhya Pradesh, and Rajasthan—between April and June 2025, ranging from brutal physical violence to the denial of basic rights.[77]Such violence extends beyond weddings. In Gujarat, Dalits have been killed or assaulted merely for watching *garba* or sporting moustaches—symbols perceived as upper-caste prerogatives. In Rajasthan, Jitendra Meghwal was murdered after years of harassment for making eye contact with dominant caste men. Between 2019 and 2021, multiple Dalits in Gujarat were beaten or stabbed for keeping moustaches. Police in Rajasthan acknowledged seventy-six such attacks over the past decade involving wedding processions alone.

Water access also remains violently policed. A Dalit boy in Rajasthan was beaten to death in 2022 for touching a pitcher.[78] Similar assaults have occurred in Gujarat and Uttar Pradesh—children flogged, students beaten, and adults murdered simply for drinking water from public sources.[79]

In 2016, four Dalits in Gujarat's Una were publicly flogged for skinning a dead cow—a caste-imposed task now reclaimed with dignity but met with violent reprisal.

These are not isolated incidents but symptoms of a

systemic order, as documented by Human Rights Watch and the National Dalit Movement for Justice. Even minor gestures—wearing footwear, sitting on chairs, riding cycles—can provoke violence or social boycott in caste-dominated areas.

Logic of the Statecraft: A Failure Foretold

How could the persistence of caste in independent India not have been foreseen by the galaxy of 300-odd stalwarts in the Constituent Assembly? That the Congress had been shaped by Gandhi's worldview—wherein caste as a system was not inherently problematic and only untouchability was condemned—is well known. Gandhi maintained that untouchability was a moral perversion, not intrinsic to Hinduism, and upheld the ideal of *varna*, albeit spiritualized and purged of birth-based inequality. Yet, toward the end of his life, Gandhi had begun to speak more directly against caste discrimination.[80]

Why then did Jawaharlal Nehru, a self-avowed modernist who disagreed with Gandhi on issues like *khadi*, village self-sufficiency, and the centrality of religion in politics, not challenge the caste order more forcefully? Nehru, unlike Gandhi, viewed caste as a social evil and championed scientific temper and rationalism.[81] However, he remained politically cautious. Conservatives like Sardar Patel and Rajendra Prasad, less inclined toward social radicalism, held considerable sway, but Nehru was hardly without influence. His reluctance hints at a deeper political calculus.

One plausible reason was the fear that dismantling caste would destabilize Hindu society. Caste had long been the organizing principle of Hindu social life; its sudden removal risked unrest in a fragile new nation. For many Hindus living in poverty, caste provided a sense of order and identity. Abolishing it might have led to perceived social chaos. Moreover, the Congress leadership—drawn largely from upper-caste backgrounds—had internalized caste hierarchies and derived security from them.[82]

Only Dalits, newly politicized under Dr. Ambedkar's leadership, could meaningfully demand caste annihilation. Yet even among them, reservations created hesitation. This was evident in the response to Ambedkar's 1956 call for mass conversion to Buddhism: while thousands converted, many retained their Scheduled Caste status out of fear of losing constitutional benefits.[83] Around the same time, Ambedkar announced the formation of the Republican Party of India (RPI). After his death, SCF leaders delayed renaming the party until after the 1957 elections to preserve access to reserved seats. Even post-conversion, Dalits continued to rely on caste-based privileges—revealing a deep anxiety about losing constitutional safeguards.[84] Ambedkar's silence on the critique that untouchability could not be abolished without dismantling caste reflects a strategic compromise.

But did reservations necessitate the preservation of caste? Not necessarily. If conceived as exceptional provisions for an exceptional group—as they initially were under colonial rule[85]—reservations for SCs were delinked from the traditional caste. The 1936 Government of India (Scheduled Castes) Order had already formalized untouchable castes as an administrative category, distinct from Hindu religious caste.[86] As such, the entire scheme of affirmative action would be unaffected by the abolition of caste. Even the extended scheme to the STs did not require caste to live. First, because the tribals did not have caste; and second, like the Untouchables, they also were grouped under a new administrative category of Scheduled Tribes.

The new rulers, it seems, wanted caste to live. Unlike the 1936 schedule created with a huge investment in extensive survey undertaken by the colonial government, which therefore was largely frozen, they kept the newly issued schedules reviewable by the political process. They also provided for some kind of affirmative action for the "Backward Classes," actually the castes. Unlike the definitive criterion of untouchability for the SCs and the somewhat loose but still plausible one—being tribes—for the STs, they lazily conceived "social and educational backwardness" as the criterion to identify these castes in future. In a backward country like India, there was perhaps no caste that could not potentially claim this backwardness. This ambiguity potentially opened the floodgates for caste mobilization. Castes, then withering under capitalist modernity, were effectively transplanted into the fertile ground of democratic representation. They were not just preserved—they were reborn as constitutional castes.

Universal adult suffrage and the adoption of the first-past-the-post (FPTP) electoral system structurally reinforced caste identities by making electoral success dependent on consolidating caste-based vote banks. The choice of FPTP was not ideologically neutral; it was adopted despite significant debate in the Constituent Assembly. A fuller discussion of these debates—and their implications for Dalit political representation—follows in the next chapter. For now, it is enough to note that the system entrenched caste identities by aligning democratic participation with localized, majoritarian arithmetic.

Since caste was deeply conflated with Hinduism, its survival ensured the survival of religion itself. As we will see in chapter 6, the new rulers crafted a uniquely Indian version of secularism—without explicitly naming it—that allowed religious identities to persist under the veneer of progressive reform. The abolition of untouchability and the proclamation of secularism gave the appearance of rupture from the colonial state, even as its underlying mechanisms of social control remained intact. Religion and caste were the proven tools for colonial "divide and rule" policy. As they had served colonial rulers in governing a divided populace,[87] the postcolonial rulers ensured they survived, despite their wearing a face of progressiveness.

Colonial governance had already trained Indians to think in terms of caste and religion. Though the Congress initially enjoyed political monopoly, it remained a party of the ruling classes—urban elites, upper castes, and emerging capitalist groups—despite Gandhi's mass mobilization.[88] However, in the absence of any close challenger, it projected itself as the nationalist party and attracted support across classes, castes, regions, and other social identities.

With the halo and charisma of the freedom struggle behind it, the Congress enjoyed a virtual monopoly in the electoral arena during the first three general elections. In 1952, it secured 44.99 per cent of the votes and won 364 seats—roughly 74 per cent of the Lok Sabha. The distant second was the Communist Party of India (CPI) with 16 seats (3.3 per cent) and 3.29 per cent of the vote. By vote share, however, the Socialist Party stood second with 11 per cent, but it won only 12 seats (2.45 per cent).

In the 1957 election, the Congress further consolidated its dominance, increasing its tally to 371 seats (75.1 per cent) and raising its vote share to 47.78 per cent. The CPI again emerged as the second-largest party by seats, securing 27 (5.47 per cent) and nearly tripling its vote share to 8.92 per cent. By vote share, the Socialist Party—now renamed the Praja Socialist Party—polled 10.41 per cent, but managed only 19 seats (3.85 per cent).

In the 1962 elections, the Congress experienced a slight dip, winning 44.70 per cent of the votes and 361 seats (73 per cent). The CPI once more emerged as a distant second, both in vote share and seat share, at 9.94 per cent and 5.87 per cent respectively.

By the mid-1960s, the electoral monopoly of the Congress began cracking. After the 1962 debacle against China, Nehru's death, and the backlash triggered by land reforms and the Green Revolution, the Congress's social coalition began to fray. The Shudra caste peasants, empowered economically as rich farmers by these policies, began demanding a bigger share of the political pie. The Congress's failure to accommodate their aspirations turned them into adversaries. It resulted in making electoral politics increasingly competitive, pushing parties to rely on vote banks based on primordial identities of caste and religion. Caste, once a feudal relic, was now constitutionally modern—a category sustained by the state to play a new role in statecraft.

Dalits, long positioned as the social reference point that affirmed Shudra superiority in the village hierarchy, faced renewed subjugation with the advent of capitalist agrarian relations ushered in by the Green Revolution. With the collapse of the old jajmani system of interdependence, they were transformed into rural proletariat, increasingly dependent on wage labour controlled by a new class of rich Shudra farmers. This class not only accumulated economic power but also appropriated the ideological mantle of Brahmanism from the former upper-caste landlords, (whom they displaced) deploying it to dominate, discipline, and violently suppress Dalits.

The contradiction between capital and labour found existing caste fault lines through which it could manifest, frequently erupting in brutal atrocities. The 1968 massacre of Dalits in Kilvenmani in Tamil Nadu marks the beginning of this phenomenon. Crucially, these developments cannot be separated from the constitutional order that, even while formally guaranteeing rights, preserved the caste structure and institutional arrangements within which such violence continued unabated.

Legal Infrastructure for Abolition of Untouchability

A plethora of acts has been enacted for implementation of Article 17 in course of time:

- The Protection of Civil Rights Act, 1955.
- The Scheduled Castes and the Scheduled Tribes (Prevention of Atrocities) Act, 1989, and the Scheduled Castes and the Scheduled Tribes (Prevention of Atrocities) Rules, 1995. They were amended multiple times to address gaps in implementation, judicial dilution, and to strengthen protections for Dalits and Adivasis—most notably in 2015, 2016, and 2018.
- The Employment of Manual Scavengers and Construction of Dry Latrines (Prohibition) Act, 1993.
- The Prohibition of Employment as Manual Scavengers and Their Rehabilitation Act, 2013, and rules thereof
- Acts and regulations in force in different states to

prevent alienation of land belonging to SCs/STs. In some states such provisions exist in the Land Revenue Code.

- Acts in different states for restoration of alienated land to SCs and STs.
- Other acts like the Child Labour Act, Bonded Labour Act, etc.

We may just focus on caste atrocities, manual scavenging, and bonded labour to assess effectiveness in terms of curbing manifestations of untouchability.

To address the rampant caste-based discrimination and the inadequacy of the Indian Penal Code, 1860, the Government of India enacted the Protection of Civil Rights Act, 1955 (originally the Untouchability [Offences] Act). Commonly referred to as the PCR Act, it criminalized the practice of untouchability. Key provisions include:

- Section 4: Prohibits denial of access to public places and transport.
- Section 5: Bars refusal of essential services on caste grounds.
- Section 6: Protects the right to pursue any profession or attend religious/social functions.
- Section 7: Penalizes the justification or propagation of untouchability.
- Section 8: Prescribes punishments from one to six months' imprisonment and/or fines up to ₹500.

- Sections 10 and 10A: Make offenses cognizable and noncompoundable, and hold public servants accountable for inaction.

While the PCR Act marked an important legal recognition of caste-based exclusion, it proved insufficient in deterring atrocities.

To strengthen protections, the government enacted the Scheduled Castes and Scheduled Tribes (Prevention of Atrocities) Act, 1989 (POA Act). Unlike the PCR Act, the POA Act directly addresses a wide range of caste-based atrocities—including land dispossession, forced labour, public humiliation, sexual violence, and social boycotts. Key features include:

- clear definitions of "atrocities" against SCs/STs;
- a partial shift in the burden of proof to the accused;
- establishment of special and exclusive special courts;
- appointment of special public prosecutors;
- amendments in 2015 and 2018 expanding offenses and removing prior sanction for prosecuting public servants;
- provisions for legal aid, rehabilitation, and victim compensation.

The POA Act recognizes caste violence not as isolated incidents but as systemic assaults on the dignity and rights of historically oppressed communities, making it a cornerstone of India's legal commitment to social justice.

Yet enforcement remains glaringly inadequate. According to the National Crime Records Bureau (NCRB), atrocity cases against Scheduled Castes rose from 42,793 in 2018 to 57,582 in 2022—a 35 percent increase over five years. With the resurgent religious ethos of the Hindu majority systematically fuelled by the current regime, there has been a clear surge in atrocity cases since 2014. A comparison of the nine-year period before 2014 with the nine years after shows that the average number of atrocities per annum jumped from 32,494 to 45,622—an astounding increase of 40.40 per cent.[89] The scale of violence becomes starker when broken down by specific crimes. In 2022 alone, 954 Dalits were murdered and 4,241 Dalit women were raped—averaging nearly three murders and twelve rapes per day in India.[90]

These figures starkly expose the deep disconnect between constitutional promises and lived realities.

Manual Scavenging

The Prohibition of Employment as Manual Scavengers and Their Rehabilitation Act, 2013, represents a significant legislative effort to eliminate caste-based indignities. It bans manual scavenging in all forms, prohibits insanitary latrines, mandates mechanized cleaning, and requires protective gear for sanitation workers. Crucially, it emphasizes rehabilitation through cash assistance, housing, loans, and other socioeconomic support, while also holding violators—both private and public—legally accountable. Vigilance committees at state and district levels are mandated to oversee implementation.

Despite its provisions, manual scavenging continues, often fatally. In September 2023, the Social Justice Ministry commissioned a study into hazardous cleaning deaths, which analysed the circumstances surrounding 54 such deaths in 17 districts across eight States and Union Territories that occurred in 2022 and 2023. Government data shows 150 people across the country died due to hazardous cleaning in 2022 and 2023.[91] As of November 2023, 714 out of 766 districts claimed to be manual scavenging-free. Yet over 400 deaths occurred between 2018 and 2023 due to septic tank and sewer cleaning—activities legally prohibited. In 2023 alone, 49 deaths were reported, with Rajasthan (10), Gujarat (9), and Maharashtra and Tamil Nadu (7 each) topping the list.

In July 2024, Union Minister Ramdas Athawale reported 377 such deaths between 2019 and 2023 but simultaneously denied the existence of manual scavenging—a claim contradicted by Section 2(1)(g) of the Act, which defines the practice as any manual cleaning of excreta without safety gear.[92]

In Maharashtra, the state admitted to 81 deaths and disbursed in Maharashtra, the state . These figures expose the gap between legal framework and ground reality, revealing systemic neglect and continued reliance on Dalit labor for hazardous tasks meant to be mechanized. The urgent need remains for robust enforcement, safe sanitation systems, and genuine commitment to constitutional dignity and equality.[93]

While the government stayed in denial, at least 30 manual scavenging deaths have already been reported in 2025, including four in Delhi. Despite the official claim that manual scavenging is banned, these deaths continue because there is neither proper mechanization nor basic safety gear. A recent social audit found that over 90% of workers who died in sewers lacked adequate protective equipment.[94]

Judicial Interventions

Courts have repeatedly intervened to bridge the gulf between law and practice. In *Safai Karamchari Andolan v. Union of India* (2014), the Supreme Court held that unsafe manual scavenging violated Article 17 and ordered ₹10 lakh compensation for each death since 1993, while warning of criminal liability for negligent officials. In *S. Sekar v. State of Tamil Nadu* (2022), the Madras High Court noted the ongoing deployment of manual scavengers despite the ban and directed a time-bound mechanization plan.

Activism, especially by Safai Karamchari Andolan under Bezwada Wilson, continues to expose the state's denial. Despite the 2013 Act criminalizing such employment, prosecutions remain rare, and judicial reminders of official responsibility underline broader institutional failures in upholding caste justice.

Bonded Labour

Despite Article 17 and the Bonded Labour System (Abolition) Act, 1976, bonded labour remains widespread, particularly in sectors where caste hierarchy, informal employment, and debt-based recruitment dominate. The law criminalized bonded labour on paper but never dismantled the structural conditions that sustain it—usurious credit, landlessness, caste dominance, and collusion between employers and local officials.

Field studies expose the caste dimension clearly. Research in Uttar Pradesh brick kilns and Karnataka's sugarcane sector shows that Dalits and Adivasis constitute over 85% of bonded workers, often tied by advances as low as ₹5,000–₹20,000. Workers rarely escape because employers control wages, movement, and police access. Rehabilitation schemes are a joke—compensation is delayed for years, and prosecutions almost never succeed. Conviction rates remain abysmal, often below 5%.

Empirical evidence is stark. The NHRC's nationwide survey with the Labour Ministry (2009–2012) estimated over 8.4 lakh bonded labourers, with Tamil Nadu, Karnataka, Andhra Pradesh, Uttar Pradesh, and Odisha as major concentrations. More recent data from rescue operations reinforces continuity: the Ministry of Labour reported over 30,000 officially "released" bonded labourers between 2017 and 2023, while civil society groups like the International Justice Mission documented over 11,000 rescues in Tamil

Nadu's brick kilns and rice mills alone in the same period. The 2023 GSI estimates that on any given day in 2021, there were 11 million people living in modern slavery in India, the highest number of any country.[95] Between April 2024 and January 2025, 246 individuals were rescued—80 percent in Tamil Nadu. In Andhra Pradesh, several cases were reported, including families released from bondage in Palnadu. Legal action followed some rescues, yet enforcement and rehabilitation remain inconsistent, exposing deep-rooted structural exploitation.

The truth is blunt: the Act abolished bonded labour legally, but the state never enforced it. The economic model of many rural industries still depends on it, and officials often look the other way. The result is a system that survives through caste power, debt bondage, and state apathy.

Child Labour

Child labour in India cannot be understood merely as an economic compulsion; it is structurally rooted in the caste system. Historically, caste determined occupational roles, relegating Dalit and other marginalized communities to stigmatized, manual, and poorly paid work. This hereditary linkage of caste and occupation meant that children born into these communities were socialized into labour from an early age, often as part of family-based survival strategies. The stigma attached to caste-based occupations—such as manual scavenging, leather work, waste collection, or agricultural servitude—ensured that these families remained confined to informal and exploitative sectors, where child labour is most prevalent. Thus, caste operates as a mechanism that reproduces labour vulnerability across generations, making child labour a structural consequence rather than an episodic phenomenon.

The weakening of traditional jajmani relations did not liberate Dalit and marginalized households; instead, the shift toward capitalist agrarian production intensified their dependence on wage labour. With no landownership and limited economic mobility, children became an integral part of household labour strategies, supplementing income through agricultural work, brick kilns, domestic labour, or small workshops. Bonded labour systems, which disproportionately trap Dalit families, further pull children into intergenerational debt bondage, normalizing their presence in exploitative workplaces. Even where legal prohibitions exist, caste-based hierarchies ensure that violations go unreported or unpunished, as employers belong to dominant caste groups who command local power structures.

Access to education remains a crucial site where caste and child labour intersect. Children from lower-caste backgrounds face systemic discrimination in schools—ranging from segregation, humiliation, and teacher bias to infrastructural neglect in marginalized localities. These hostile environments lead to high dropout rates, pushing children into labour. Poverty alone does not explain this trajectory; the social exclusion embedded in caste relations ensures that education does not function as a reliable avenue of mobility for many marginalized children. The consequence is a self-perpetuating cycle where lack of schooling reinforces labour vulnerability, and labour in turn curtails educational opportunities.

Despite constitutional guarantees and legislation such as the Child and Adolescent Labour (Prohibition and Regulation) Act, child labour persists at alarming levels, with contemporary evidence showing a disproportionate representation of Scheduled Caste and Scheduled Tribe children in the labour force. Recent surveys in states like Telangana report that 80–90 per cent of identified child labourers belong to SC/ST communities, underlining the caste character of the phenomenon. Official narratives that attribute child labour solely to poverty obscure the deep structural inequalities that sustain it. In reality, child labour survives because caste ensures a steady supply of cheap, compliant labour, protected by social norms and shielded by weak enforcement.

Therefore, child labour in India must be understood as a caste-mediated institution that reproduces social hierarchies. Legal bans and welfare schemes have limited impact when they fail to dismantle the caste structures that create and sustain labour exploitation. Without confronting caste-based exclusion, discrimination in education, and the continued dominance of caste elites over local labour markets, child labour will remain embedded in India's social fabric.

Structural Failure of Article 17 Enforcement

Despite a dense legal and judicial framework built around Article 17, untouchability remains entrenched in everyday life. The Constitution banned the practice but did not abolish caste itself, allowing the social and institutional structures that sustain discrimination to persist. The very institutions meant to enforce the law—the police, judiciary, and bureaucracy—are deeply marked by caste consciousness. Their routine refusal to register cases, downgrading of offences, delays in trial, and sympathy for dominant caste perpetrators ensure that legal protections remain largely symbolic. When the state machinery shares the worldview of those who uphold caste hierarchy, constitutional guarantees offer little relief to Dalits.

For the first few decades after independence, caste assertion appeared muted in public life, not due to genuine transformation but because the nationalist-socialist ethos made open caste display socially unacceptable. Caste continued to dominate village power structures and private domains, waiting for conditions favourable to its resurgence.

The neoliberal turn from the 1990s unleashed economic insecurity and intensified competition over land, jobs, and resources. Dominant agrarian castes, enriched through earlier economic reforms, reacted aggressively to Dalit mobility and political assertion. The rhetoric of meritocracy enabled them to deny caste privilege while opposing affirmative action, sharpening social tensions. The Mandal reservations, a byproduct of caste-based political mobilization, gave a major fillip to caste contestations.

Under the current Hindutva regime, caste has returned to the public sphere with new confidence. Revivalist Hindu nationalism glorifies traditional social order, providing ideological cover for caste hierarchy. Open display of caste markers, segregation in temples and villages, and caste-based mobilization have become widespread. Social media has further amplified these assertions. The state, aligning with dominant caste interests, often protects perpetrators and grants them impunity.

The result is a society where caste is more visible, aggressive, and socially sanctioned than before. Legal prohibitions have failed because the underlying caste structure remains intact. India today is arguably more casteized than ever, with constitutional ideals routinely subverted by social reality and state complicity.

Chapter IV

Reservation in Political Representation

The British strategy of "divide and rule," though never formally declared, crystallized after the Revolt of 1857 into a deliberate policy of reinforcing divisions—religious, caste, and ethnic—to maintain colonial dominance. Queen Victoria's 1858 Proclamation promised religious noninterference but entrenched communal identities by pledging protection of group customs. As Thomas Metcalf and others note, colonial governance after 1857 sought to secure their rule by anchoring Indian society within fixed categories of caste and community, thereby ensuring that no unified political movement could emerge against them.[96]

British tools of classification—census, legal codes, and electoral systems—progressively recast Indian society into rigid categories. From the 1871 census onward, Indians were compulsorily sorted by religion and caste, transforming fluid identities into fixed administrative labels. The colonial state further hardened these distinctions through separate personal laws and the imagination of India as a land of communities rather than citizens.

The most far-reaching political effect of this approach came with the Morley-Minto Reforms of 1909, which introduced separate electorates for Muslims. Voters were now segregated by community, formalizing religious identity in electoral politics. This model was extended to Sikhs, Christians, and eventually Dalits under the Communal Award of 1932. By the 1920s, British officials were openly advocating communal separation to forestall national unity. Viceroy Linlithgow warned of "the danger of Hindu-Muslim unity,"[97] while the Home Department sought to isolate Muslims from the Congress and court princely states and minorities.

Colonial policies communalized politics, culminating in Partition. As Francesca Jensenius (2022) notes, it was the British who institutionalized identity-based quotas, creating a framework within which all political leaders were inadvertently pushed to operate. This "representational governance" set the stage for political claims rooted in group identity, producing competitive demands for quotas across communities.[98]

Dr. Ambedkar saw in this colonial framework an opportunity to claim political space for Dalits. Disillusioned with Hindu reform efforts after the Mahad Satyagraha in 1927[99], he turned his focus to political representation, stressing the separate identity of Dalits from Hindus. His call for conversion was attuned to this strategy. In 1919, before formally entering public life, he had already argued before the Southborough Committee that Dalits were entitled to separate electorates, just as Muslims had been granted under the Morley-Minto Reforms.[100]

At the Round Table Conferences (1930–32), his efforts led to Dalits being granted separate electorates under the Communal Award of 1932. However, Gandhi, by going on a fast unto death against this award, forced him into signing the Poona Pact, which, inter alia, replaced separate electorates with joint electorates and reserved seats—thus retaining caste Hindus'political control over Dalit representation.

This structure, codified in the Government of India Act, 1935, and later the Indian Constitution, trapped Dalit politics within a framework Ambedkar could not dismantle—even as chairman of the Drafting Committee. Over time, he came to see this as perpetuating Dalit subordination under the guise of inclusion.

Ambedkar's engagement with the colonial representational system was a strategic move to secure an authentic political voice for Dalits. His success in winning separate electorates was meant to ensure that Dalits would elect their own representatives, not proxies of dominant castes. This gain, however, was lost in the Poona Pact—a compromise that may have been unavoidable. But it should have prompted a search for a new strategy. Instead, Dalits became increasingly invested in the system of political reservations. What was intended as a means to liberation gradually turned into a trap, diverting attention from the larger goal of annihilating caste and anchoring Dalit politics within the limits of electoral representation.

Constitutional Provisions

The Constitution adopted reservations for Dalits in legislative bodies from the Government of India Act, 1935. It extended these provisions to the Adivasis, creating a similar schedule for them. Articles 330 and 332 provide for reservation of seats in proportion to their population in a state or union territory.

Article 334 of the Constitution had originally required the reservation of seats to cease in 1960, but this was extended to 1970 by the Eighth Amendment. The period of reservation was extended to 1980 and 1990 by the Twenty-third and Forty-fifth Amendments respectively. The Seventy-fifth Amendment extended the period of reservation to 2000. The period of reservation was further extended to 2010, 2020, and 2030 by the Seventy-ninth, Ninety-fifth, and One Hundred Fourth Amendments respectively. It was done almost automatically, without any palpable demand from Dalits. It clearly proved that these reservations served the interests of the ruling classes.

It is notable that the system of political reservations for Dalits was entirely the result of Ambedkar's own efforts. He first secured separate electorates for the Depressed Classes at the Round Table Conferences, and later—under the coercive circumstances of the Poona Pact—negotiated with Gandhi to retain reservations, though now within joint electorates. The compromise more than doubled the number of reserved seats, creating initial enthusiasm among Dalits. However, Ambedkar soon realised the structural flaw: without separate electorates, Dalit representatives would remain dependent on caste-Hindu voters and parties, undermining independent Dalit political agency. Disillusioned, he began demanding the annulment of these very reservations, recognising that the Poona Pact had effectively neutralised the political gains he had originally secured.

Ambedkar's demand to annul the Poona Pact emerged clearly by the mid-1940s, particularly in his 1945 memorandum to the Cabinet Mission and subsequent speeches, where he argued that the Pact had fatally undermined Dalit political autonomy by tying their representation to caste-Hindu majorities and making Dalit legislators dependent on Congress-controlled electorates. He attempted to reverse its terms in the Constituent Assembly, but even as Chairman of the Drafting Committee he lacked both the political strength and institutional backing to do so. The Assembly was overwhelmingly dominated by the Congress, and Ambedkar remained a marginal figure within it, reliant on Congress support even to retain the limited safeguards he was negotiating. Consequently, he was compelled to accept the Poona Pact framework of reserved seats and incorporate it into the Constitution as a pragmatic compromise, even while continuing to denounce the Pact publicly as a historic blow to Dalit political independence. He agreed to reservations only for an initial period of ten years, never anticipating that they would be perpetuated indefinitely by the ruling classes.Reserved SC/ST seats create a loyal bloc for mainstream parties. Data suggest that many Dalit MPs act more like blind supporters of their parties than as champions of their communities. According to IndiaSpend's analysis of PRS Legislative Research data, SC/ST MPs from the BJP spoke only about 10 times a year during the 15th Lok Sabha (2009–14).[101] In parliamentary committees too, SC/ST legislators often have a limited voice.[102] And even speaking or representation is not a guage of representation of their constituency.

Reservations via Articles 243D and 243T (Panchayati Raj and Municipalities)

- These articles mandate the reservation of seats for SCs and STs in local self-government institutions (panchayats and municipalities) in proportion to their population.
- They also reserve positions for SC/ST women in these bodies.

While reservations have ensured that Dalits occupy roughly 15 percent of seats in legislatures—matching their population share—this numerical representation has not translated into real political empowerment. Dalits can contest both reserved and general seats, but victories in general constituencies remain exceedingly rare. In the Lok Sabha, their presence has stagnated around 84 of 543 seats; in state assemblies, about 625 of 4,099. Even at the grassroots level—across over 2.8 lakh local bodies—their representation rarely exceeds 17 percent.

Crucially, where reservations do not apply, Dalit representation plummets, exposing entrenched caste biases in Indian politics. In the Rajya Sabha, which has no reserved seats, Dalits constitute only about 7 percent of members. Cabinet inclusion has also been poor: just 8.33 percent in 2019, falling to 6.57 percent in 2021 and inching up to 10 percent in 2024. Ministers of State fared slightly better but remained underrepresented. In 2019, only two Dalits won from 412 general Lok Sabha seats. Party ticket distribution was telling—BJP fielded just two Dalits in general constituencies, Congress only three. The 2024 elections saw SC representation edge up marginally from 15.5 percent to 15.8 percent, underscoring continued dependence on reserved seats.

At the local level, panchayats and municipalities—often hailed as democratic cornerstones—are deeply shaped by caste dominance. Far from being inclusive, they frequently serve as instruments of elite capture. SC representatives routinely face marginalization: being excluded from meetings, denied cooperation, made to sit separately, or distanced by the physical location of offices—all of which undercut their effective participation.

Though political representation was central to the Dalit movement's demands, its transformative potential was never clearly theorized. There was an implicit assumption that shared identity would translate into advocacy for Dalit interests. In practice, Dalit representatives remain fragmented, tied to ruling-class parties that nominate and finance them, and largely unaccountable to their communities. Rather than acting as autonomous voices, they often function as loyal agents of their political patrons.

Over seven decades of electoral democracy, as seen above, Dalit MPs and MLAs have rarely raised their voices on issues of caste violence or systemic exclusion. The extension of SC reservations—originally a temporary provision—has continued without significant demand from Dalits themselves, reflecting their utility to dominant parties more than any structural progress for the community.

The Limits of Political Reservations

Evidence from India and abroad shows that while political reservations increase descriptive representation, they rarely deliver substantive empowerment. Mala Htun's (2016) research on Latin America demonstrates that quotas often lead to numerical inclusion without improving the socioeconomic position of marginalized groups. Similarly,

Chauchard and Jensenius (2023) note that SC reservations in India have been shaped by ambiguous and contradictory expectations. Their design discourages assertive advocacy by Dalit politicians, entrenching rather than dismantling structural barriers.

At the local level, studies of Panchayati Raj institutions reveal that Dalit sarpanchs rarely prioritize Dalit interests. Electoral compulsions push them into multi-caste alliances, and the rotation of reserved seats incentivizes short-term patronage. Party affiliations further dilute accountability, shifting loyalty from community to party. Whether Dalit or upper caste, incumbents often favour their own caste during their brief tenure. Overall, research shows that reservations do not systematically translate into pro-Dalit policy outcomes.

While SC reservations have enabled Dalit participation in electoral politics, they have done little to alter caste hierarchies or material deprivation. Structural constraints and party dependence render Dalit politicians ineffective as agents of change. Instead, reservations sustain a symbolic inclusion that maintains Dalit faith in the system without challenging the status quo. For ruling parties, they are a tool of political co-optation—securing Dalit votes while offering limited accountability or reform.

That said, reservations can open modest avenues of state access. At the village level, SC sarpanchs can function as intermediaries between Dalit communities and administrative systems, improving access to welfare and justice—though only marginally, and within a context still dominated by caste bias and bureaucratic gatekeeping.

At higher levels, representation is even more diluted. The vast scale of constituencies detaches MPs and MLAs from their constituents, who must navigate intermediaries—brokers, fixers, party workers—to access state power. These networks privilege those with money or influence, deepening political inequality and rendering representation hollow for many Dalits. The persistence of such structures calls for electoral reforms that democratize access and enhance institutional accountability.

Political reservations can slowly influence caste attitudes, but change is uneven and often superficial. Dominant groups may begin to tolerate SC leadership out of expediency, not conviction. The symbolic presence of Dalits in power may challenge social hierarchies in perception, but rarely in substance.

The Folly of Representation

The paradox that representatives from oppressed groups often serve dominant interests is well established in political theory. Robert Michels's "iron law of oligarchy" argues that all democratic structures develop elite hierarchies that alienate leaders from the masses they claim to represent.[103] In this light, Dalit politicians—though elected—often align with ruling elites rather than champion their own communities.

Antonio Gramsci's notion of transformismo similarly

explains how ruling classes absorb dissent by incorporating subaltern elites, neutralizing their radical potential.[104] In India, reservations have created a political class of Dalit leaders who rely on upper-caste support and party patronage, making them agents of the status quo. Even Ambedkar's proposed separate electorates might not have averted this tendency toward elite capture and dependence.

Frantz Fanon's warning about the postcolonial national bourgeoisie—which imitates colonial elites while maintaining structural inequalities—finds eerie resonance in India's Dalit leadership.[105] Partha Chatterjee's concept of "political society" captures how marginalized groups engage the state not through rights but through brokerage and informal negotiation, often mediated by their own leaders.[106] These intermediaries, far from being autonomous representatives, tend to trade community interests for individual advancement.

The system of political reservation has entailed what may be called the "domestication" of Dalit leadership: instead of confronting caste power, it has been absorbed by it.[107] Political reservations, in this view, have enabled the emergence of Dalit elites without enabling Dalit emancipation.

It is striking that few have critically examined the fact that political reservations in India are deeply tied to the first-past-the-post (FPTP) electoral system—a colonial legacy. This system, with its winner-takes-all logic, often marginalizes minorities in communally diverse societies, as they are structurally disadvantaged in competing against numerically dominant groups. Reservations, then, function less as instruments of justice and more as political concessions offered by the majority to secure minorities' buy-in. Rather than challenging communal divisions, the system reinforces them by institutionalizing identity-based representation. In India, this dynamic has played out with remarkable consistency.

Were There No Options?

Notwithstanding minor changes, SC reservations have certainly not lent Dalits a voice, let alone transformative social progress. Their impact on political competition is neutral or negative; material benefits are weak or inconsistent; and while they do improve state-citizen interactions and intercaste relations, the overall effect remains limited. A key reason lies in institutional incentives. Since SCs are a minority even in reserved constituencies and SC candidates compete against each other, elected SC politicians must appeal to non-SC voters to secure electoral success. This reduces their incentive to strongly advocate for Dalit-specific issues.[108] Additionally, party leadership—often dominated by non-SCs—restricts opportunities for assertive Dalit leaders to rise within the system.[109]

The political representation granted to Dalits in the Constitution led to the emergence of a sizable Dalit political class. However, the money-driven FPTP electoral system offers little scope for independent Dalit politics, forcing this class to seek alliances with ruling-class parties. Over time, these alliances have turned Dalit representatives into instruments of dominant political forces, ensuring their survival and prosperity within the system while sidelining the broader Dalit struggle for emancipation. The entire network of Dalit politicians becomes dependent on ruling-class patrons, serving their electoral and policy strategies rather than advancing Dalit interests. The net effect is the enrichment of this political class at the cost of genuine Dalit empowerment, ultimately reinforcing the very hierarchies that reservations were meant to challenge.

Would Dalit representation in politics not be possible without reservation? The answer may be in the negative. Dalits constitute the biggest and a fairly conscious vote bank, which no political party within the prevailing framework can afford to ignore. There is no reservation in the executive (cabinet) for Dalits, but many Dalits routinely find berths in ministries in central as well as state governments. Notably, there have been quite a few Dalits who became chief ministers of states[110], some became governors, and even presidents (K. R. Narayanan and Ram Nath Kovind). It is a different matter that none could do much for Dalits. Muslims, Christians, and Sikhs had political reservations during colonial times but gave them up during the making of the Constitution. They do get elected without reservation. The question of whether they truly represent their respective communities is moot—but the same applies to the SCs with reservation.

The extant political reservation was sought to be annulled by Dr. Ambedkar and was condemned as "Chamcha Raj" by Kanshi Ram, as it only produced political stooges out of Dalits for the ruling classes.[111]

Would separate electorates have helped? There is no definitive answer, though Dalit sentiment has generally favoured the idea—primarily because it was strongly upheld by Dr. Ambedkar and later by Kanshi Ram. Separate electorates might have facilitated Dalit-specific political mobilization and offered symbolic autonomy in political representation. However, even within such a system, there was no guarantee that authentic Dalit voices would prevail. Under the FPTP system, electoral outcomes are often shaped more by the resource-intensive strategies of political parties than by the preferences of voters. Dominant parties, with their disproportionate control over money, muscle, and media, could still sideline genuine Dalit candidates in favor of more pliable figures.

In this context, separate electorates may have served more as a symbolic concession than a structural corrective. A more meaningful solution would lie in adopting an electoral system that reduces the role of money, enhances representation for all, and ensures equitable access to state institutions. Yet such reforms have never been explored by Dalit leaders. They have been expectedly and deliberately excluded from mainstream political discourse by ruling-class parties.

While reservations have secured a measure of quantitative

representation for Dalits—nominally proportional to their population share—this has translated into little substantive power. The structural logic of the electoral system continues to tie Dalit representatives to the patronage networks of dominant parties and the state, rendering them politically dependent and often voiceless. What Dalits have lacked is an autonomous political formation that reflects their lived realities and formulates strategies rooted in their specific historical and social experience. The FPTP system fundamentally impedes such political transformation. This raises a critical question: Is there truly no alternative to the FPTP electoral system, which is not only structurally biased against the resource-poor majority but also profoundly ill-suited to India's vast social diversity and aspirations for genuine democracy?

Separate Electorates and Structural Alternatives

Separate electorates, supported by Ambedkar and later Kanshi Ram, may have offered symbolic autonomy, but they would not have guaranteed authentic leadership. Under FPTP, electoral outcomes are dictated by resource-rich parties rather than community aspirations. Even separate electorates might have yielded pliable candidates over radical ones. Thus, while emotionally resonant, they may have functioned more as symbolic concessions than structural correctives.

What is truly needed is an overhaul of the electoral system—reducing the role of money, enabling proportional representation, and ensuring institutional equity. Yet such reforms have rarely been on the agenda of Dalit leaders or mainstream parties. Despite numerical parity through reservations, Dalits remain tethered to dominant-party patronage networks, denying them substantive political agency.

The Case for Proportional Representation

Proportional representation (PR) aligns legislative seats with vote shares, thereby reducing vote wastage and ensuring fairer representation. Unlike FPTP, where a party can form government with arithmatic majority, PR translates electoral will more faithfully. For instance, the BJP won 37.4 percent of the vote in 2019 but claimed 56 percent of Lok Sabha seats; similar distortions recur across states. PR curbs this distortion and prevents the marginalization of smaller or dispersed communities. Even when a party has a genuine majority of the vote, it cannot afford to ignore the opposition. In India's FPTP system, no party has ever crossed that threshold, yet the country has twice been pushed to the edge of authoritarian rule—first under Indira Gandhi and now under Narendra Modi. Just a single win of political power at the centre by the BJP in 2014 with a mandate of less than one-third of voters has enabled its leader to assume totalitarian powers and transform the country into an illiberal democracy or an outright fascist state. This would have been impossible with a PR system, as there would be an opposition that carried the mandate of two-thirds of voters.

Moreover, PR disincentivizes electoral manipulation. Under FPTP, dummy candidates, vote splitting, and horse-trading thrive. Campaigns become contests of cunning, not principle. PR shifts the focus to programmatic, ideology-driven politics and supports parties that represent specific constituencies—regional, caste-based, or ideological—without hardwiring social divisions into the electoral process.

PR also helps convert caste and community identities into political interest groups, offering a path to inclusion without deepening caste consciousness. By reducing the need for identity-based quotas, it could gradually support the project of caste annihilation. Its flexibility allows adaptation to diverse societies like India, and it could have been a more fitting choice during constitution making. Worldwide, most political thinkers favour PR systems, and empirically the better-performing democracies are based on this system. Countries that used FPTP as the legacy of their colonial past are rethinking its outcome. New Zealand's 1996 shift from FPTP to mixed-member proportional (MMP) following public backlash demonstrates that structural reform is possible—and effective.

Indeed, most developed democracies today use some form of PR, recognizing its capacity to reduce distortion and promote inclusive governance. Unlike FPTP's frozen formula of "winner takes it all," the PR system offers an option to customize it to specific needs. It is a framework within which infinite variants are possible. India's continued reliance on FPTP is increasingly out of sync with its democratic aspirations and complex social fabric.

PR System in the Constituent Assembly

The debate around proportional representation (PR) in the Indian Constituent Assembly reveals a tension between democratic pluralism and the imperatives of political consolidation. Despite the clear democratic advantages of PR, its adoption was ultimately bypassed during the framing of the Indian Constitution. This was not due to a lack of awareness or advocacy, but due to political unwillingness of the Congress which wanted a strong one party government which can never be guaranteed by PR.

The idea of PR had surfaced right at the beginning of the consideration of electoral system in India. In the deliberations following the Montagu-Chelmsford Reforms of 1919, the select committee on the Government of India Bill had recommended a study of PR's applicability to Indian conditions. However, no such study was conducted. The colonial government could not be much interested in democracy in India, particularly when PR was just rejected in its home country. In India, its calculus clearly favoured FPTP that created an impression of sharing power without actually needing to do so.

In the United Kingdom, the Royal Commission on Electoral Systems (1910) had recommended the adoption of PR—specifically the Single Transferable Vote (STV)—as a more equitable alternative to the First-Past-the-Post (FPTP) system. The Commission's report highlighted several structural defects in FPTP, including the distortion of electoral mandates, the under-representation of minorities, and a high number of wasted votes. These issues were seen as undermining the democratic principle that legislative representation should mirror the distribution of public opinion. The Commission proposed that STV could better reflect the plurality of political views and reduce the arbitrary majoritarianism inherent in the prevailing system.[112]

Despite the merits of the recommendation, the British Parliament declined to implement PR. The rejection was driven primarily by the political self-interest of the dominant parties—namely, the Liberals and Conservatives—who stood to lose their electoral advantages under a more proportional system. There was also a pervasive fear that PR would produce fragmented parliaments and unstable coalition governments, echoing the perceived failures of continental European polities.[113] Additionally, the technical complexity of STV and its unfamiliarity were cited as potential sources of voter confusion.[114] The broader political culture, steeped in conservative constitutionalism and institutional inertia, further hindered any transformative change.[115] As Vernon Bogdanor notes, while the Commission's case for reform was intellectually robust, its recommendations were politically inconvenient and thus "quietly shelved."[116]

It was this report that Babasaheb Ambedkar would refer to in his argument against the PR system in the CA debate.

PR did figure in the CA in a significant way, though it was hardly meaningfully discussed. Somnath Lahiri, the sole Communist member, emerged as its strong advocate, arguing it would ensure representation of all political parties—ideological, regional, or communal—commensurate with their electoral support.[117] He was not alone. Members like Rajkumari Amrit Kaur, Hansa Mehta, and D. H. Chandrasekharaiya also supported PR or cumulative voting as a noncommunal mechanism to secure minority integration without relying on separate electorates or reserved seats.[118]

The demand for separate electorates and reservations for minorities was weakened by Partition. The Minorities Sub-Committee, in its July 1947 report, rejected Ambedkar's proposals for intercommunity vote thresholds and cumulative voting, choosing instead joint electorates with reserved seats for SCs and STs, subject to a ten-year review. This decision, while nominally a minority safeguard, institutionalized the FPTP system within single-member constituencies, marginalizing broader proportional claims.

The Congress Party's resistance to PR was steadfast. Proposals by Minoo Masani for cumulative voting and PR-STV were dismissed.[119] Despite endorsements from provincial leaders like P. Subbaroyan, B. G. Kher, and Hansa Mehta, Congress rejected PR as too complex for India's illiterate masses.[120]

Muslim members, in particular, persistently argued for PR. On July 17, 1947, Mahboob Ali Baig critiqued the assumption that parliamentary systems are inherently democratic, insisting that democracy requires institutional representation of all sections in both legislature and executive. Citing Switzerland's consensual model, he advocated PR to preserve India's pluralist character.[121]

Calls for PR continued. On July 28, 1947, Haji Abdul Sattar Haji Ishaq Sait proposed electing the Council of Ministers through PR-STV, which Jawaharlal Nehru summarily rejected, warning it would yield a "feeble government." This reflected the leadership's broader fear that PR would fragment the political centre and weaken executive power.[122]

On August 28, 1947, D. H. Chandrasekharaiya presented a detailed case for PR using STV and SNTV, drawing from examples like Northern Ireland and South Africa. He refuted the complexity argument by pointing out that universal adult franchise had already been adopted despite mass illiteracy.[123]

The most sustained case for PR came from Kazi Syed Karimuddin, who, on November 5, 1948, condemned joint electorates with reserved seats as tokenistic. He warned of majority-backed proxies replacing genuine minority representatives and pushed for a PR system with multi-member constituencies and plural voting. Notably, he cited Ambedkar's *States and Minorities* (1947), which had advocated a nonparliamentary executive to protect minorities.[124]

On January 4, 1949, Karimuddin argued that PR was essential to avoid "tyranny of the majority." He emphasized that PR ensured every vote counted and could render communal reservations obsolete while still securing minority inclusion. He cited the United States, United Kingdom, and Ireland as examples where FPTP distorted the popular mandate.

Several others echoed this logic. K. T. Shah emphasized PR's capacity to reflect diverse political opinions rather than merely communal identities.[125] Baig reiterated that if PR was suitable for the Council of States, it should also apply to the Lok Sabha.[126] On November 8–9, 1948, Baig, along with Hussain Imam[127] and B. Pocker, again defended PR, with only Pocker voicing concern over its complexity.

On May 25, 1949, Zahirul Hasnain Lari invoked the successful use of PR in Ireland, Belgium, and Switzerland to argue that disenfranchising minorities contradicted democratic principles. Quoting Lord Acton, he called PR "profoundly democratic." Without it, he warned, minorities would be excluded from meaningful political participation.[128] Lari refuted the claim that PR was akin to separate electorates, emphasizing that PR was a fair and tested system that had worked in many democratic countries.[129]

Yet, the dominant leadership held firm. On May 26, 1949, Sardar Patel rejected PR as impractical for India's scale and diversity, citing illiteracy and administrative hurdles. Members like Anantswamy Ayyangar,[130] Renuka Ray[131],

L. Krishnaswamy Bharati[132], and Thakur Das Bhargava opposed PR, believing it would revive communal electorates. H. J. Khandekar, an SC member, feared PR might deepen communal divisions, while V. I. Muniswami Pillai defended distributive voting as a unifying tool. Others, including R. K. Sidhwa, Durgabai Deshmukh, and Shiban Lal Saxena, dismissed PR due to perceived operational complexity.[133]

Even within reserved constituencies, PR's weakening was noted. On July 30, 1949, V. I. Muniswami Pillai criticized the draft Constitution for removing STV provisions from the Council of States, warning this would dilute Scheduled Caste representation.[134]

By the end of the debates, disappointment was palpable. On November 21, 1949, Karimuddin lamented that in the hope of PR, he had earlier supported the abolition of reserved seats. Now, with both PR and reservations abandoned, he said, "the privileges and rights which we had enjoyed for the last 60 years exist no more, and we depend on the good sense of the majority."[135]

The Scheduled Castes Federation (SCF), in its 1944 Political Demands, had clearly demanded PR and separate electorates, alongside reservations in the executive and local bodies. Yet Ambedkar, by the time of the Draft Constitution, aligned with the Congress-led consensus, abandoning these demands. He spiritedly opposed PR in the CA, citing voter illiteracy[136], risk of political instability due to party fragmentation, and its purported incompatibility with parliamentary democracy—pointing to Britain's rejection of PR in 1910.[137] He further argued that PR would undermine minority representation by not guaranteeing fixed quotas[138], revealing his anxiety to protect Dalit political reservations. However, many of his arguments against PR lacked strong justification.[139]

According to Abhay Datar, the clearest and most reasoned defence of PR came from D. R. Gadgil, a noted economist, who rejected the notion that single-member constituencies ensured political stability. Drawing on interwar France, he demonstrated that such systems often failed to do so. Gadgil emphasized that in a diverse country like India, PR was better suited to fairly represent religious, linguistic, and social minorities. He argued that hopes of political integration via single-member constituencies were misguided and likely to entrench majority dominance.[140]

Gadgil highlighted that, unlike reservations—which required statutory backing—PR could organically enable minority inclusion. He even proposed a list system for consideration but acknowledged that his proposals would not appeal to the Congress leadership, which was invested in maintaining a centralized, majoritarian regime. Gadgil's critique laid bare the Congress's oligarchic impulse: a reluctance to accommodate electoral systems that might decentralize power or empower dissenting voices.[141]

In the end, despite vocal support from Socialists, Communists, and liberal nationalists, the Assembly settled on FPTP with limited reservation for SCs and STs. The Draft Constitution of November 1948 institutionalized joint electorates, single-member constituencies, and rejected PR or cumulative voting for the Lok Sabha. In the final debates of August 1949, all reservations except those for SCs and STs were abolished. Muslim members like Pocker Sahib Bahadur, Muhammad Ismail Sahib, and Z. H. Lari pleaded for either PR or continuation of minority reservations—but to no avail. Syed Saadulla warned that without mechanisms like PR, India risked becoming an oligarchy.[142]

FPTP in India's Plutocracy

Ultimately, India retained the FPTP system despite its inherent flaws in a diverse polity. The main reason behind its acceptance, as noted by D. R. Gadgil, was that the Congress leadership wanted a strong one-party government, which only FPTP could provide.[143]

The FPTP system has transformed elections into a game of money and manipulation, privileging party-driven electoral strategies over genuine voter choice. Rather than fostering substantive debates on policies and governance, elections have been reduced to contests of outspending and outmaneuvering opponents.

Parties deploy an array of strategies, including fielding dummy candidates to split opposition votes, orchestrating propaganda blitzes, staging massive rallies with hired crowds, bribing local community leaders, and distributing freebies to lure voters. There is a built-in incentive for keeping the masses poor, illiterate, and vulnerable. These strategies require enormous financial resources, which in turn provide space for moneyed interests in electoral politics. Corporate funding has become the backbone of election campaigns, with businesses funnelling vast sums into parties in anticipation of favourable policies once their beneficiaries assume power. It naturally leads to a capital-driven system sans any moral compunction.

The 2019 Lok Sabha election, reportedly the world's most expensive, exemplified this trend. According to a report by the Centre for Media Studies, an estimated ₹55,000 crore (approximately $8 billion) was spent on the elections, surpassing even the cost of the U.S. presidential race.[144] In the 2024 Lok Sabha elections, analysis by the Association for Democratic Reforms (ADR) revealed that about 20 percent of candidates had criminal cases against them, while approximately 31 percent were crorepatis (candidates with assets over ₹1 crore), with average assets of ₹6.23 crore. Post-election, ADR again analyzed the self-sworn affidavits of all 543 winning candidates in the Lok Sabha 2024 elections. According to the report, a striking 93 percent are crorepatis. The chance of winning for a crorepati candidate in the Lok Sabha 2024 was 19.6 percent, whereas it was only 0.7 percent for a candidate with assets less than ₹1 crore. There has been a significant increase in the number of MPs with declared criminal cases since 2009. Out of the 543 winning candidates, 251 (46 percent) have declared criminal cases. Comparatively,

233 (43 percent) MPs had declared criminal cases in 2019, 185 (34 percent) in 2014, and 162 (30 percent) in 2009.[145]

This financial nexus has led to massive corruption and the criminalization of politics, where electoral success increasingly depends on wealth rather than merit or public service. The FPTP system has, in effect, turned Indian democracy into a plutocracy—a system where power is dictated by those who control the purse strings. In this system, not only Dalits but the entire lower class is effectively disenfranchised.

A PR system would certainly dampen these developments, if not curb them altogether. Without any reservation, the SCs, as a sizable political community, would have their own representation and more, because many other minor communities would have made common cause with them. There is an intrinsic push within PR systems to create interest groups and thereby dampen primordial identities in politics. This would have led to erosion of caste consciousness and to the annihilation of caste. Unfortunately, this was not to be.

Chapter V

Reservations in Educational Institutions and Public Employment

It may be surprising to note that reservations in education and public employment—though today seen as central to Dalit progress—did not constitute the primary demand of the Dalit movement. It figured first in a formal way in the demands before the Simon Commission. These provisions emerged as a by-product of political reservation. The Poona Pact of 1932, which replaced separate electorates with reserved seats, included a Congress commitment to ensure fair representation of the Depressed Classes in public services, with due consideration to their educational qualifications.[146] This clause, having been part of the Government of India Act, 1935, became the basis for reservations in educational institutions and public employment. Initially, what emerged was a preferment system—if a qualified SC candidate was available, he or she would be preferred over others. It was only during Ambedkar's tenure as Labour Member in the Viceroy's Executive Council (1942–46) that this principle was transformed into a formal quota system, which was incorporated into the Constitution.

The constitutional provisions that grant SCs reservations in educational institutions and public employment are as follows:

1. Educational Institutions

- Article 15(4): Introduced by the First Amendment (1951), it enables the state to make special provisions for the advancement of socially and educationally backward classes (SEBCs), including SCs and STs. This forms the constitutional basis for reservation in educational institutions for SCs.
- Article 15(5): Inserted by the Ninety-third Amendment (2005), it allows the state to make special provisions for the admission of SCs, STs, and SEBCs in private educational institutions (excluding minority institutions under Article 30[1]).

2. Public Employment

- Article 16(4): Empowers the state to make provisions for the reservation of appointments or posts in favor of any backward class of citizens, including SCs and STs, that is not adequately represented in state services.

- Article 16(4A): Inserted by the Seventy-seventh Amendment (1995), it allows for reservation in promotions for SCs and STs in government employment.
- Article 16(4B): Ensures that the total number of reserved promotions (including carried-forward vacancies) does not violate the ceiling of 50 percent in a single year.

Related Provisions

Article 335 states that the claims of SCs and STs must be taken into account, consistently with the maintenance of administrative efficiency, in matters of public employment. It recognized the need for SC representation in government jobs, though less explicitly structured than in the final Constitution.

Reservation in the Constituent Assembly

The founding moment of the Indian republic was marked by an explicit acknowledgment of caste as a fundamental axis of discrimination.

The Sub-Committee on Fundamental Rights drafted Article 10(3) (later Article 16[4]) to allow reservations for backward classes underrepresented in public services, based on the state's opinion. The Minority Rights Sub-Committee's report, addressing various minority claims—including those of SCs—recommended in Article 296 (later Article 335) that such claims be considered in public appointments, provided administrative efficiency was maintained—a term introduced here but left undefined.

The Constituent Assembly Debates engaged extensively with the moral, legal, and political rationale for instituting reservations in educational institutions and public employment for the SCs, STs, and other backward classes. At the heart of the pro-reservation discourse was Dr. Ambedkar, who argued forcefully for reparative justice to redress centuries of caste-based oppression and exclusion: "The Depressed Classes were not only not allowed to enter the public services but were also prohibited from pursuing ordinary education," he stated, urging the Assembly to "make special provisions to overcome this handicap[147]." Supporting this, K. M. Munshi cautioned that without constitutional safeguards, dominant castes would continue to monopolize opportunities, thereby reproducing structural inequality.[148] K. Santhanam noted that reservation for SCs was "not a privilege but an act of compensation for centuries of oppression and humiliation[149]." Similarly, Sardar Hukam Singh emphasized that reservations were essential for ensuring representation of marginalized communities in governance, asserting, "If the Scheduled Castes are not given a fair share in public employment, the administration will remain a monopoly of a few privileged classes[150]." Jaipal Singh, speaking for tribal communities, lamented their historical neglect and insisted that reservations were crucial for their educational and economic uplift: "Unless they get reservations, they will never catch up with the rest of India[151]."

These claims were situated within the broader constitutional framework, with Dr. Rajendra Prasad invoking the Preamble and Article 46 of the Directive Principles to argue that substantive equality required affirmative action.[152] T. T. Krishnamachari rooted the idea in Gandhian ethics, stating that "Mahatma Gandhi himself fought for the rights of the Depressed Classes[153]," while S. Nagappa pointed to the domination of Brahmins in government services as evidence of caste monopoly that reservations aimed to dismantle.[154] R. K. Sidhva added that education was key to social mobility, and reservations were a matter of justice, not charity.[155] Dr. Ambedkar similarly argued that reservations were essential to allow SCs entry into administration and political life, so they could protect their rights and assert their voice in governance.[156] He clarified that such measures were transitional: "I agree that the remedy (reservations) may not be the best, but it is necessary for some time to level the playing field[157]."

Despite broad support, some members expressed concerns. H. V. Kamath, for instance, worried about the implications for administrative efficiency, stating, "We should not sacrifice efficiency at the altar of social justice[158]." R. V. Dhulekar argued that merit and equality before law were paramount, fearing that reservations could institutionalize caste distinctions rather than abolish them.[159] Naziruddin Ahmad raised objections on grounds of constitutional consistency, cautioning that reservations, if continued indefinitely, could contradict the principle of equal opportunity.[160] These dissenting voices reflected anxieties about efficiency, meritocracy, and the potential permanence of what was intended as a temporary measure. Nonetheless, the Assembly ultimately endorsed reservations, embedding them in Articles 15(4), 16(4), and 335 of the Constitution as instruments of justice and inclusion.

The language of "backward class" and "adequate representation" was contested for its vagueness. Members like Sardar Hukam Singh and R. M. Nalavade warned that these undefined terms could lead to the inclusion of relatively advanced groups, diluting the spirit of the provision.[161] Nonetheless, the Assembly left it to the state's discretion to identify and support genuinely marginalized communities.

Ambedkar insisted that reservations were not privileges but remedies—a constitutional guarantee to redress structural exclusion.[162] However, even this framing was insufficient. Merely equating representation with population share does not compensate for centuries of denied opportunities; it risks freezing historical deficits and carrying them forward indefinitely.

Marc Galanter (1984) argues that reservations in India are designed to compensate for the structural and historical disadvantages suffered by certain communities, particularly Dalits. Unlike affirmative action in the United States, which is largely framed in terms of individual discrimination, India's reservation policy is grounded in the recognition of group-based disabilities embedded in the social fabric.[163]

Christophe Jaffrelot reinforces this perspective in *India's Silent Revolution*, contending that reservations have been among the few effective mechanisms enabling a measure of upward mobility for Dalits. While caste-based inequality remains deeply entrenched, the rise of a Dalit middle class in some regions is largely attributable to access provided by reservations in education and public employment.[164]

The rationale behind reservations extends beyond mere representation. It is rooted in the ambition to disrupt the social order that normalizes exclusion. Education and employment are crucial pathways to social respect, economic independence, and political agency. As Ambedkar aptly put it, "It is not enough for a man to be elected, he must be educated[165]."

Post-independence data underscores the continued necessity of such measures. Despite constitutional guarantees, SCs still suffer from high dropout rates, underrepresentation in higher services, and entrenched discrimination within institutions.

The Uneven Politics of Reservation

Unlike most other provisions in the Indian Constitution, reservation policies in educational institutions and public employment for SCs touch directly upon the material conditions of Dalit life. These measures aim to rectify deep historical injustices of caste exclusion by facilitating access to state-sponsored opportunities long monopolized by upper castes. Consequently, these reservations have been the most contested and resented by the so-called "General Category," a nomenclature that masks entrenched privileges of caste elites under a veneer of neutrality.

The irony is sharpened by the temporal asymmetry built into India's constitutional design. Educational and employment reservations were never time-bound and remain subject to periodic policy review, while political reservations were explicitly temporary—initially set to expire after ten years under Article 334. As Jaffrelot notes, this permanence has benefited mainstream parties, who often use SC-reserved constituencies to insert compliant Dalit leaders and contain dissent, undermining genuine representation.[166]

In contrast, material reservations face ongoing judicial and political scrutiny. Supreme Court rulings like *Indra Sawhney* (1992) and *M. Nagaraj* (2006) have imposed stringent conditions—proof of backwardness and administrative efficiency—rarely applied to political quotas. Galanter has shown that while educational and job reservations have had redistributive effects, they also invite backlash from dominant castes.[167]

Peril of the Premise

The dominant rationale behind reservations for SCs in India has, since its inception, been anchored in the idea of their historical "backwardness"—the assumption that they are a socially and educationally disadvantaged group requiring state support to become equal members of society. This framing constructs Dalits as though they were intrinsically deficient. Such a construction has had far-reaching implications—not only for the political legitimacy of reservations but also for the psychological and social standing of Dalits within the Indian polity.

The Government of India Act, 1935, granted reservations to SCs in the name of historical exclusion. It justified this on the premise that SCs were an exceptional community that remained backward not due to inherent inferiority but as a result of systemic discrimination and social ostracism. However, when these provisions entered the Indian Constitution under Articles 15(4), 16(4), and 46, there was a subtle but consequential shift in moral and political emphasis. Rather than framing reservations as a remedy for societal failure, the constitutional language—and more importantly, its political reception—came to tacitly cement the notion that Dalits were inherently "backward" and thus required extraordinary concessions.

This shift has led to two significant consequences. First, it reinforced casteist prejudice in the social imagination—fostering the perception that Dalits are an inferior people who may deserve sympathy but not rights, and that they are being unfairly elevated by a state driven by vote-bank politics. Second, it has imposed a profound psychological toll on

Dalits themselves, who are often made to feel that they are undeserving or second-rate. What was originally conceived as a measure of social justice thus becomes a marker of social deficit.

More fundamentally, the logic of self-termination—conceptually embedded in affirmative action worldwide, where such measures are seen as transitional and intended to become obsolete once their objective, equality, is achieved—finds no clear articulation in the Indian Constitution. While political reservations under Article 334 were explicitly time-bound (albeit repeatedly extended), educational and employment reservations remain open-ended. This absence of a clearly defined exit clause paradoxically reinforces the idea that Dalits are perpetually incapable of achieving parity with others, thereby normalizing their supposed inferiority.

The Constituent Assembly debates that supported these reservations often articulated them as reparations for historical wrongs and as a means to bring Dalits on par with others. Yet both premises were flawed. The first was incorrect because there was no element of reparation in the provisions—only a vision of getting them representation in the present, limited to their share in population. The second was also misplaced: there was nothing in the constitutional text to suggest that past deficits would automatically be wiped out over time. Moreover, objections about reservations undermining "merit" rested on a self-serving and narrow definition of merit. These criticisms implicitly assumed that reservations were a blanket ticket to public services without any requirement of qualification.

The truth is that reservations were not necessitated by any intrinsic deficiency among Dalits but by the structural failure of Indian society, which continues to be hostile to the ideal of equality. Rather than viewing reservations as compensation for Dalit inadequacy, they should be understood as a countervailing measure to overcome societal deficiencies and entrenched caste prejudices. It is not Dalit individuals who must "catch up" with society, but the social order itself that must expunge its caste biases and catch up with the ideals of a modern, egalitarian polity. In this light, the state, through reservations, is not favouring a minority but disciplining a historically unjust majority. The stigma of deficiency would have been borne by the larger society and not Dalits. And Dalits, for their part, would have tried to transcend the limitation of reservation and avail themselves of larger opportunities in larger society instead of developing vested interests in reservations. The state would have accelerated the change with educative campaigns. Viewed this way, the policy of reservation could have been a powerful instrument to achieve the larger goal of annihilating caste—instead of perpetuating it, as it often does today.

The premise of the extant reservation system, deeply embedded in public discourse, has not only reinforced casteist prejudices but also fostered a pervasive resentment among non-Dalits, who perceive reservations as an unjust usurpation of their entitlements. This misplaced premise ends up producing "an image of Dalits as inferior beings eternally dependent on state benevolence," rather than as victims of entrenched social injustice.[168]

The backlash generated by the discourse around reservations has often translated into real-world violence. In rural India, Dalits—motivated by Ambedkar's exhortations and the promise of reservations—have increasingly turned to education as a means of advancement. This has enabled some to acquire formal education and secure employment in government and public sector jobs. In contrast, rural dominant castes, long entrenched in farming and agro-based occupations, have shown little cultural inclination toward education. The upward mobility of Dalits—historically considered inferior—has triggered envy and resentment among dominant-caste communities. Although a stray Dalit individual might be visible in this progress, there has been a widespread catalytic cultural transformation within Dalit communities, fostered by the spread of education and the legacy of Ambedkar's movement, which necessarily manifests in growing assertions of civil rights. This transformation has had two major consequences: first, it made Dalit youth unavailable as farm labour, driving up rural wages; and second, it disrupted the traditional caste-based social order. Since the notion of dominant-caste superiority was premised on Dalit subordination, these shifts have been perceived as threats to the established hierarchy. Reservations have become the scapegoat for these broader changes, often deemed illegitimate by dominant castes.

Atrocities against Dalits, particularly in rural areas, are frequently provoked by the perception that they have overstepped their socially ordained status under the protective umbrella of state policy. These incidents are not merely episodic but symptomatic of a deeper social pathology wherein the assertion of Dalit rights is construed as transgression. Ironically, the Dalits most vulnerable to such violence are often those who remain in agrarian villages, untouched by the actual benefits of reservations, yet punished for the perceived elevation of their brethren. This is the consequence of irrational attribution of reservation to the caste and not to the individual, as it should be.

Moreover, the beneficiaries of reservations—those who manage to enter the professional and bureaucratic classes—often find themselves caught in a peculiar sociological predicament. Economically and professionally, they belong to the middle class, yet they remain largely excluded from its cultural and social networks due to the enduring stigma of caste. Simultaneously, they are distanced from their own caste communities, which continue to live in conditions of economic deprivation and social precarity to which they would not like to return. As a result, they occupy what may be called a "Trishanku" position[169]—neither here nor there. This liminal existence entails profound psychological costs, including chronic anxiety, identity dissonance, and a persistent sense of inadequacy despite visible markers of success. In response to this dislocation, many seek solidarity and affirmation by forming SC/ST associations and sociopolitical organizations like BAMCEF. Yet the underlying psychological burden remains, often rendering them defensive and reflecting a deep-drawn inferiority complex, inhibiting their ability to fully realize their potential.

Another largely unnoticed phenomenon stems from two faulty assumptions: first, that Dalits constitute a homogeneous community; and second, that the benefits of reservation, though accruing to an individual or their immediate family, somehow uplift the entire caste. The combined effect of these misconceptions has manifested in growing competition among Dalits for limited reservation opportunities—whether in coveted educational institutions or public employment. Those who benefited earlier continue to enjoy a structural advantage. Their children, having access to better schooling and a more enabling cultural environment, are positioned more competitively than the children of those left behind. This intra-community disparity has been erroneously interpreted as an uneven distribution of reservation benefits among the various constituent castes within the Scheduled Castes. This framing has been conveniently appropriated by the political class to stir intracaste rivalries and promote the dubious remedy of subcategorization of reservation quotas. Even sections of the intellectual class, under the guise of concern for the "deprived" subcastes, have endorsed this politically expedient but flawed solution. What remains overlooked is that the root of the problem lies in the original conception and formulation of the reservation policy itself—not in its distribution among subcastes.

As reservations extended into second and third generations, a more confident Dalit professional class has emerged—less burdened by the inferiority complex of their predecessors, yet still shadowed by caste. Many among them constitute a sort of Dalit diaspora, replicating older forms of cultural assertion in elevated, urban contexts. Their upward mobility often translates into a celebratory embrace of Dalit identity. However, this assertion is increasingly disconnected from the lived realities of the broader Dalit population, which today faces a crisis arguably deeper than before.

This detachment illustrates a paradox: rather than annihilating caste, reservations have in some ways reinforced it by institutionalizing caste within a framework of redress. As Marc Galanter noted in *Competing Equalities*, while reservations were intended to overcome disadvantage, they have produced a competitive hierarchy of entitlements, generating new caste tensions rather than dissolving old ones.[170] The model of "compensatory discrimination" has thus reproduced, rather than transformed, the social order.

Conceived as a compensatory mechanism, the policy fails to truly compensate for the vast historical injustices suffered by Dalits. Instead, it merely attempts to secure their rightful place in the present. Lacking a sound conceptual foundation, it has neither resolved the structural roots of caste nor prevented its reconfiguration in new forms.

All policies entail costs to produce benefits. While reservations have facilitated the rise of a Dalit middle class, they have also brought significant psychological, social, and organizational costs—and have, in important ways, compromised the goal of caste annihilation.

Mild worries about merit, national cohesion, and administrative efficiency were voiced in the Constituent Assembly, but there was no disagreement on the necessity of reservations for the Scheduled Castes. As H. V. Kamath expressed a hope that before the ten-year mark from the Constitution's commencement, "we shall do away with this stigma of any caste being scheduled."[171] Yet such objections were in the minority. K. T. Shah and others insisted that equality without equity was hollow and that affirmative action was essential to redress historical injustices.[172] Thakur Das Bhargava argued that while educational reservations could aid Dalit uplift, political and employment-based quotas were vital to dismantling entrenched caste prejudice.[173] T. J. M. Wilson stressed that caste persisted even after religious conversion, calling for the inclusion of Dalit Christians.[174] Jerome D'Souza described reservations as "functional representation," necessary for integrating the historically excluded into the democratic fold.[175]

Some, like Chaudhari Ranbir Singh, urged moving from caste-based to economic and occupational criteria, fearing that codifying caste would reify it.[176] But the Assembly ultimately recognized that in India, caste and economic deprivation are deeply intertwined and cannot be separated.

Outcome over Seven Decades

Education is a vital instrument for economic mobility and social transformation. Beyond enabling livelihood, it cultivates rational thinking, secular values, and social integration. It also influences demographic behaviour, including fertility rates, marriage age, and workforce participation. Higher education levels among women, for instance, are strongly associated with delayed marriage, reduced fertility, and improved child health outcomes.

For Dalits, affirmative action in education and public employment has been one of the few effective tools for upward mobility. Unlike political reservations, which have had limited impact, educational and job quotas have enabled a visible shift in Dalit presence across professions and regions. These policies have provided not only economic security but have also challenged entrenched social hierarchies, fostering a more egalitarian society.

At independence, India inherited a deeply stratified education system that mirrored and reinforced its social hierarchy. Rural government schools were little more than shelters—often without proper buildings, trained teachers, sanitation, teaching materials, or measurable learning standards—while urban elites had access to well-funded municipal, missionary, and private institutions offering

English-medium instruction, laboratories, libraries, and pathways to higher education and employment. This layered structure ensured that children's educational trajectories were determined from the outset by caste, class, and location. Instead of dismantling these divisions, post-independence policy largely preserved them. The Kothari Commission (1964–66) explicitly identified this inequality and proposed a Common School System to ensure that all children, irrespective of background, attended the same neighbourhood schools. The political establishment—dominated by elites who benefited from exclusivist schooling—ignored it. Over time, the growth of private schools, aided by state neglect of government education, widened the gap further. Structural inequity in schooling thus became entrenched at the formative stages, reproducing social inequality rather than alleviating it, and locking generations of marginalised communities into disadvantage.

This historical layering did not remain static; it hardened. The failure to implement the Kothari Commission's call for a Common School System ensured that educational access continued to follow social rank rather than democratic ideals. What should have been dismantled was instead reinforced, allowing structural inequalities to deepen. By the 1990s, with neoliberal reforms and shrinking public investment, privatization accelerated this stratification. Elite urban schools surged ahead, while rural government schools—where most Dalit children study—remained starved of resources. In utter neglect of the Commission's recommendations, the tiered system became even more acute, systematically pushing Dalits to the bottom of the educational hierarchy.

Since the 1990s, the market-driven turn in education has pushed Dalits further to the margins. As private capital flooded the sector, education became a lucrative business for political entrepreneurs who converted black money into sprawling colleges, universities, and school chains. According to UDISE+ 2021–22, nearly 48% of all schools in India are now privately managed, up from about 20% in the early 1990s. Private schools account for over 38% of total enrolment, but more than 70% of Dalit children remain in government schools. In higher education, AISHE 2020–21 notes that 78% of colleges and 60% of total enrolment are in private institutions, while in professional and technical education privatization is even more extreme, with over 80% of engineering and medical colleges privately owned. Meanwhile, public spending has stagnated at around 3% of GDP, far below the 6% target recommended by the Kothari Commission.

These institutions now dominate the landscape, outstripping government provision in both scale and influence, but they function as exclusive enclaves—pricing, language, admission norms, and cultural environments effectively shut out SC/ST students. With public schools collapsing and private education unaffordable, Dalit children are trapped in a deteriorating government system that offers little mobility. The result is a harsh sorting mechanism:

elites buy opportunity, while Dalits inherit deprivation, reinforcing caste hierarchy under the veneer of merit and market efficiency.

Private schools and colleges, especially those offering English-medium education, overwhelmingly serve upper-caste elites. Even in rural areas, costly private schools have become status symbols for the neo-rich dominant castes, while government schools—where Dalit children are concentrated—remain underfunded, understaffed, and academically weak. This structural divide traps Dalit students in substandard institutions, eroding their academic foundations and narrowing their future employment prospects.

Although reservations exist in public universities, the rapid expansion and dominance of private higher education—where affirmative action provisions do not apply—effectively nullifies these constitutional safeguards. As access to quality education becomes increasingly tied to the ability to pay, Dalits find themselves excluded from the very pathways that promise upward mobility, entrenching the cycle of caste-based disadvantage under the guise of choice and merit.

Structural economic barriers—poverty, poor-quality schooling, and social exclusion—prevent Dalits from accessing meaningful education. Reservations alone cannot bridge this gap. Without robust public investment, regulation of private institutions, and targeted financial support for marginalized students, education will continued to reproduce caste hierarchies rather than dismantle them.

Seven decades later, access to education and employment remains unequal. SC students make up only 14.2 percent of higher education enrolment, far below their population share (AISHE 2020–21), and dropout rates at the secondary level remain disproportionately high (U-DISE+ 2021–22). Sociological research confirms the enduring power of caste in shaping life outcomes. Christophe Jaffrelot notes that caste continues to mediate access to education, jobs, and mobility even after liberalization.[177] Marc Galanter similarly warns that in the absence of structural safeguards, reforms risk reproducing old hierarchies rather than dismantling them.[178]

Reservations in Government Employment

Despite being hailed as the constitutional instrument for Dalit empowerment, reservations in government employment have delivered meagre returns while imposing a disproportionate stigma. The public sector—the only domain where reservations formally apply—covers barely about 4 percent of India's workforce, compared to 32 percent in China and 15–25 percent in major Western economies. Within this narrow space, the 15 percent SC and 7.5 percent ST quotas translate into benefits for only about 0.6 percent of SCs and an even smaller proportion of STs. In exchange for this pittance, Dalits have been branded as a "pampered" group, subjected to lifelong humiliation, and portrayed as dependent on state charity, even though the policy has scarcely altered their collective socio-economic position.

Worse, the institutional culture of the public sector has been structurally hostile. Dominated by upper-caste elites, it views Dalit employees as inherently inferior and admits them reluctantly. Discrimination manifests in placements, work assignments, training access, and promotions, resulting in Dalits being concentrated in low-impact roles and excluded from decision-making positions. As oversight mechanisms exposed these patterns, managements adapted by elevating a handful of compliant Dalit employees as tokens to showcase "meritocratic fairness," while assertive and competent individuals who challenged discrimination were punished through stagnation and hostile work environments. The outcome is perverse: the system produces demoralization and professional decay, reinforcing the very stereotypes used to marginalize Dalits, turning the public sector into a graveyard of Dalit aspirations.

Compounding this failure was a fundamental lack of imagination in policy design. Reservations never accounted for the risk that benefits would accrue repeatedly to the same small segment, creating a rising intra-caste inequality in which the already advantaged within SCs monopolized opportunities. No mechanism ensured wider dispersion or redistribution of the gains, leaving the majority untouched while producing a thin Dalit elite increasingly disconnected from their community base.

Finally, the Constitution offered no answer to the inevitable contraction of the public sector. After the 1990s, neoliberal reforms led to privatization, outsourcing, and contractualization of work. Public sector employment, which constituted nearly 69 percent of formal jobs in 1991, fell to around 32 percent by 2020, while permanent government jobs declined sharply and contractual positions surged beyond 40 percent. As most new recruitment shifted to temporary and outsourced routes where reservations do not apply, the effective domain of affirmative action collapsed. Meanwhile, the expanding private sector, operating on market logic and allergic to formal commitments to representation, accepted Dalits only selectively and continued to discriminate through hiring bias, networking barriers, and glass ceilings.

Thus, reservation policy not only failed to meaningfully uplift the majority of Dalits but also entrenched stigma, intensified internal inequality, and left the community exposed when the public sector shrank. The constitutional promise of social justice was structurally undermined from the outset, producing symbolic inclusion with negligible substantive transformation.

Although the broader failures of reservation policy are visible across sectors, the dynamics in academia are even more telling. Higher education has historically been the near-exclusive preserve of Brahminical castes, who monopolized knowledge production and institution-building. This legacy persists. Academic spaces—especially elite ones—have exhibited extreme reluctance to admit Dalits into faculty ranks, treating them as intellectual interlopers rather than equals. The result is a stark mismatch between constitutional promises and institutional realities.

The numbers expose this refusal. In 2019, only 3.47

percent of professors and a mere 0.7 percent of associate professors in forty central universities were SC/STs. As of 2021, over one-third of SC faculty posts and nearly half of ST faculty posts in elite institutions such as IITs, IIMs, and central universities remained vacant. IITs had just 1.68 percent SC/ST faculty, and IIMs an abysmal 0.23 percent—despite substantial SC/ST student enrolment. The message is clear: institutions that loudly celebrate merit weaponize it to exclude Dalits. Scholars have shown that this meritocratic rhetoric simply disguises caste privilege and maintains elite dominance.

This hostility undermines the very purpose of reservation. Instead of expanding representation, elite institutions have preserved their caste character by refusing to fill reserved positions, hiring through contractual or ad hoc routes, or redefining eligibility criteria. The outcome is a near-total failure of reservation in the sector that most shapes knowledge, leadership, and social mobility. Dalits who fight their way through education encounter a closed gate at the point of academic employment, reinforcing the belief that higher learning is not their domain.

The consequences spill outward. With academia blocking entry, Dalits face reduced opportunities and weaker incentives for pursuing higher education. Post-1990s privatization further shrank the already tiny space where reservations applied. The collapse of academic representation thus becomes both a symptom and a driver of broader exclusion, ensuring that knowledge production, institutional leadership, and intellectual legitimacy remain firmly in upper-caste hands.

Chapter VI

Secularism and Issues of Impunity

In this chapter, we consider just two features of the Constitution: (i) secularism and (ii) the statist bias that lends impunity to state functionaries vis-à-vis citizens. These features, though not directly related to Dalits, have had a disproportionately adverse impact on them.

The Constitution's version of secularism never confronted the religious foundations of caste. Instead of dismantling religious identity as a political category, it constitutionalized it through personal laws, minority rights, and the continued legal recognition of Hindu social structures. Dalits were trapped within the Hindu fold by default, with no constitutional mechanism to escape the religious identity that legitimizes their oppression. The refusal to abolish caste-based personal laws, to reform temple access fundamentally, or to outlaw practices linked to ritual purity meant that the so-called secular state continued to outsource social authority to religion. In electoral politics, this preserved the Hindu majority as a political bloc while minorities mobilized on religious lines, leaving Dalits fragmented and co-opted rather than empowered. In effect, secularism without caste annihilation only reinforced the very hierarchies it claimed to transcend.

The statist character of the Constitution compounds this injury. It privileges state interests—order, security, administrative convenience—over individual rights, giving wide impunity to police, bureaucracy, and security forces. For Dalits, who overwhelmingly face the state from the position of vulnerability—whether as landless labourers, informal workers, protestors, or accused persons—this bias has been lethal. Police atrocities, false cases, and custodial violence disproportionately target them, while officials enjoy legal shields and procedural protections that make accountability rare. When the state fails to deliver welfare, justice, or protection, Dalits have little constitutional recourse; when they assert their rights, the same state wields coercive power against them. Thus, both the incomplete secularism and the statist architecture of the Constitution structurally tilt the balance against Dalits, deepening their marginalization rather than alleviating it.

Secularism

Secularism, ironically, not to be found in the constitutional text, is routinely projected as a core constitutional value.

The word itself entered the Preamble only in 1976 through the Forty-second Amendment—introduced during the Emergency, a period that fundamentally undermined the republic's democratic foundations. India's traumatic experience of religious division, particularly between Hindus and Muslims, culminating in Partition, should have prompted a decisive constitutional break from religion as a political force. Instead, religion—historically embedded in social life as a source of solace amid misery—remained a potent fault line available for political mobilization. In Europe, secularism emerged precisely to prevent such manipulation: a firewall separating religion from politics after centuries of religious wars and clerical domination.

Secularism, at its core, denotes the wall of separation between religion and the state, ensuring that religious institutions do not direct state policy and that the state does not privilege or suppress any religion. George Jacob Holyoake, who coined the term in 1851, defined secularism as a social order grounded in reason and human welfare rather than theological authority.

Holyoake's definition reduces to a clear, blunt idea: secularism is a practical ethic devoted to improving human life in this world, using reason, science, and material means, rather than theology or promises of salvation. It treats human welfare—not God, scripture, or the afterlife—as the basis of morality. Its core commitments are: human improvement through better social and material conditions; ethics grounded in experience and reason; service to others as a civic duty; cooperation, justice, and equitable distribution of resources; sincerity and conviction based on informed judgment; treating work and social responsibility as the highest form of "religiousness" For Holyoake, secularism replaces theological authority with provable, constructive principles aimed at eliminating poverty, ignorance, and suffering here and now. It demands that inequality be corrected in this life, not deferred to a hypothetical next one.[179]

The idea of a *"wall of separation"* emerged from raw political necessity in Europe, where religion had become a source of state power, persecution, and war. Three historical trajectories converged: (1) The European religious wars (16th–17th centuries), (2) The rise of the modern state, and (3) Enlightenment political theory. Thinkers like Locke argued that religion concerned salvation, while the state concerned civil interests—life, liberty, property. If the state enforced religion, it destroyed both civic peace and genuine belief. The precise phrase comes from Thomas Jefferson's 1802 letter to the Danbury Baptists, assuring them that the U.S. Constitution's First Amendment built *"a wall of separation between Church and State."* It became constitutional doctrine only later, through American jurisprudence. The French Revolution, reacting to the Church's political power and wealth, pushed for laïcité—religion expelled from public authority entirely (Law of 1905). Secularism thus transformed from a moral philosophy (Holyoake) into a political technology: a structural barrier between state power and religious authority, designed to prevent the state from becoming the instrument of any faith.

Different historical trajectories produced different models. Charles Taylor distinguishes between laïcité, the French model that strictly excludes religion from the public sphere, and "political secularism," the Anglo-American model that maintains neutrality while allowing religious expression in public life.

The Indian model of secularism is embedded in several key constitutional articles: Article 14 (Equality before Law), Article 15 (Prohibition of Discrimination), Article 25 (Freedom of Conscience and Religion), Article 26 (Freedom to Manage Religious Affairs), Article 27 (Non-financial Support for Religion), Article 28 (Religious Instruction in State Schools), and Article 44 (Directive Principle for a Uniform Civil Code). Together, these provisions shape India's distinctive approach to secularism—a system that does not strictly separate religion and state (as in the Western model), instead seeks to provide space for the state to intervene to reform religious practices, and keeping equal distance from all religions. respecting individual religious freedoms in a pluralistic society.

India's constitutional order, however, adopts neither model. Although the Preamble now proclaims secularism, its insertion into a visionary, non-operative section makes little practical difference. The Constitution retains and manages religion rather than separating it from the state. Indian secularism does not exclude religion from public life, nor does it commit to genuine neutrality. Instead, the state actively administers religious institutions, recognizes and enforces personal laws rooted in religious doctrine, and accommodates religious customs within its legal framework. Far from erecting a barrier between religion and politics, the constitutional design kept religious identities intact and politically salient, ensuring that religion continued to shape social power and state policy.

Its comparison with the Anglo-American model may be revealing:

Key differences between Indian and Anglo-American Secularism

Aspect	*Anglo-American Model*	*Indian Model*
State–Religion Relationship	Strict separation (non-interference and neutrality); "wall of separation" (Jefferson)	Principled distance: state may intervene in religion to uphold constitutional values
Religious Freedom	Freedom *from* religion in public life; religion largely privatized	Freedom *of* religion and cultural rights, including group-based practices

Aspect	*Anglo-American Model*	*Indian Model*
State Aid to Religion	Prohibited (especially in U.S.; no funding of religious institutions)	Allowed selectively (e.g., funding of religious schools, subsidies for pilgrimages, management of temples)
Equality	Formal equality before law	Substantive equality: state may treat communities unequally to ensure justice (e.g., personal laws, minority rights)
Public Role of Religion	Religion confined to private sphere (especially in U.S.)	Religion visible in public sphere, including festivals, symbols, and public offices taking oaths in God's name

India defines its own version of secularism by three tenets:

(1) *Sarva Dharma Sambhava*, which translates as equal respect for all religions, not strict separation;

(2) *Principled Distance*[180], meaning the state maintains a flexible engagement with religion to protect rights and correct injustices; and

(3) Interventionist Secularism—the Indian state can regulate or reform religious institutions (e.g.,

banning untouchability, temple entry laws), which is inconceivable in the American model.

On paper, Indian secularism presents a unique framework involving equal respect for all religions, principled distance, and state-supported religious reform. However, on careful analysis, its contradictions are exposed. In a society where 80 percent of the population identifies with Hinduism, how can the state, which itself is constituted by majoritarian elections and whose institutions are dominated by Hindus, be neutral to all religions or maintain balance between its so-called reformatory interventions? These principles, as empirical evidence shows, do not operate on a neutral or level field. Rather, they risk becoming mechanisms through which the state manages, regulates, and reinforces religious (and often majoritarian) identities. Beneath its pluralistic façade, Indian secularism may well function as a statecraft of governed religiosity—where religion is not diminished but carefully preserved and administered for political ends.

Constitution's Equivocation

Members of the Constituent Assembly (CA) representing minorities, who relinquished their demand for political reservations in favour of a secular state, expressed concerns about discrimination. They pointed out that the definition of Scheduled Castes (SCs) and Scheduled Tribes (STs) was restricted to Hindus, thereby excluding Dalit Christians and

Dalit Sikhs. For instance, T. J. M. Wilson[181] and Sardar Hukam Singh[182] raised this issue. Kazi Syed Karimuddin pointed out discrimination against Muslims in sectors such as defence and railways, contradicting the claim of a secular state.[183]

In contrast, Hindu members of the Assembly argued that Hinduism itself was inherently secular. Dr. Panjabrao S. Deshmukh, a member from the Central Provinces, for example, asserted that even if India had been declared a Hindu state, the Constitution would have remained secular because "there is no religion on earth which is more secular in character than Hinduism."[184] Similarly, Algu Rai Shastri and Shibban Lal Saxena[185] objected to the ban on religious instruction in publicly funded schools, warning that this could prohibit the teaching of Hindu scriptures like the *Gita* and *Ramayana*.[186] Such majoritarian delusions dominated constitutional discourse.

There was thus no coherent understanding of secularism among the Assembly members. None of them advocated a complete separation of religion and state; rather, they celebrated the idea of state neutrality as secularism. Brajeshwar Prasad's proposed amendment to the Preamble—"WE, THE PEOPLE OF INDIA...having resolved to constitute India into a SECULAR CO-OPERATIVE COMMONWEALTH to establish a SOCIALIST ORDER..."—was rejected.[187] Similarly, K. T. Shah's proposal to include "secular" and "socialist" in the Preamble, to read "India shall be a Secular,

Federal, Socialist Union of States[188]," was dismissed. Ambedkar ignored Shah's 'secularism' altogether. He dealt only with "socialist," arguing: "What should be the policy of the State, how the Society should be organised in its social and economic side are matters which must be decided by the people themselves according to time and circumstances. It cannot be laid down in the Constitution itself, because that is destroying democracy altogether[189]," and thereafter saying that the socialistic direction is already outlined in the DPSP: "If these directive principles to which I have drawn attention are not socialistic in their direction and in their content, I fail to understand what more socialism can be."[190]

It is ironic that despite the initial reluctance to include secularism in the constitutional text, the Indian Constitution later came to be celebrated as a model of secularism. Some even eulogize it as an innovative "Indian model of secularism."[191]

Impact on Dalits

India's model of secularism, often celebrated for its pluralist accommodation and ostensible neutrality toward all religions, in reality institutionalizes a caste-inflected framework that privileges dominant social and religious groups while systematically marginalizing Dalits. Far from functioning as a bulwark of emancipatory equality, Indian secularism serves as a technology of rule that accommodates religion while preserving the caste order rooted in Brahminical Hinduism. Nowhere is this contradiction more apparent than in the state's treatment of Dalits who convert to Islam or Christianity—religions that theoretically reject caste but whose followers in India remain entangled in its oppressive structures.

At the heart of this exclusion lies the Presidential (Scheduled Castes) Order of 1950, which restricts Scheduled Caste status—and thus access to constitutionally guaranteed reservations in education, public employment, and political representation—to Dalits professing Hinduism. This was later extended to Sikh Dalits in 1956 and to Buddhist Dalits in 1990, but continues to deny recognition to Dalits who convert to Christianity or Islam. The justification offered by the state is that caste, as a social system rooted in Hindu theology, does not exist in these religions. Yet this rationale crumbles under the weight of sociological evidence and lived experience.

Numerous studies, including those by the Sachar Committee (2006) and the Ranganath Misra Commission (2007), have shown that caste-based discrimination persists among Indian Muslims and Christians, particularly those of Dalit origin. Dalit Christians often remain in segregated parishes, perform menial jobs within church institutions, and are denied leadership positions. Dalit Muslims—often referred to as *Pasmanda*—face exclusion within the larger Ashraf (upper-caste)-dominated Islamic sphere. Despite these realities, the state maintains the legal fiction that these religions are inherently egalitarian and thus incapable of harbouring caste hierarchies.

This exclusion is not a mere oversight—it is a structural feature of the Indian secular project. The denial of Scheduled Caste status to Dalit converts is a mechanism of caste discipline: it punishes exit from Hinduism by withdrawing state protection and affirmative action. In effect, it creates a system where Dalits are allowed to resist caste only within the framework of Hinduism—preferably through movements like reformist Buddhism—but are penalized when they seek religious mobility as a form of social escape. The state thus rewards compliance with the Hindu fold while penalizing defection from it.

This dynamic became especially visible in Meenakshipuram in 1981, when over a hundred Dalits from the Tirunelveli district in Tamil Nadu converted en masse to Islam in protest against persistent caste violence and exclusion. The conversions triggered widespread political backlash. The state and Hindu nationalist organizations immediately cast suspicion on the act, raising allegations of foreign funding and coercion. An official commission was set up, and reconversion campaigns were launched. The incident demonstrated how Indian secularism accommodates Hinduism's internal reform (e.g., temple entry movements or ritual reform) but becomes anxious and even hostile when Dalit dissent takes the form of religious exit.

This contradiction points to a deeper ambiguity within the Indian constitutional framework. While Article 15(1) of the Constitution prohibits discrimination on grounds of religion, race, caste, sex, or place of birth, the 1950 Order openly violates this principle by making religious identity a criterion for eligibility for caste-based protections. Dalits within Hinduism are deemed deserving of redress, while their counterparts in Islam or Christianity are not. The law thus codifies a form of religious discrimination while cloaked in the rhetoric of caste abolition.

Such contradictions are not incidental; they reflect the ideological underpinnings of Indian secularism itself. Unlike the Western model of secularism, which seeks a strict separation of church and state, Indian secularism operates on the principle of "principled distance." The idea is that the Indian state, instead of being equidistant from all religions, engages with them selectively to promote justice, liberty, and equality. But in practice, this has resulted in inconsistent and often politically expedient state behaviour. The state intervenes aggressively in some religious domains (such as Muslim personal law or Islamic educational institutions), while remaining silent or even complicit in others (such as temple management, cow protection laws, or Hindu religious festivals).

This uneven application of secular principles often aligns with the interests of the dominant majority. As Ashis Nandy has noted, Indian secularism is less about protecting minorities than about shielding the majority's religious practices from scrutiny.[192] The state's involvement in temple rituals, allocation of funds for Hindu pilgrimages, or endorsement of festivals like Ram Navami or Diwali as national celebrations is rarely questioned. Yet when Muslim women wear the hijab in public schools—as in the Karnataka hijab ban of 2022—the act is interpreted as an affront to secular values and grounds for exclusion. As Faizan Mustafa has pointed out, this selective invocation of secularism reveals its use as a disciplinary tool rather than a liberatory one.[193]

The state's role in temple governance is equally revealing. While it maintains control over the administration and revenue of many Hindu temples through state boards, it rarely uses this authority to challenge the caste-based exclusions practiced within these institutions. Dalits are still denied entry into numerous temples across India, or are allowed entry only under the gaze of the police and the media during symbolic state-sponsored events. Temples like the Jagannath Temple in Puri or the Sabarimala Temple in Kerala continue to impose exclusionary practices, often upheld by casteist and patriarchal interpretations of religious purity. The Hindu Code Bills, passed in the 1950s to reform personal laws on marriage, inheritance, and guardianship, were limited to upper-caste norms and left untouched the economic and ritual privileges of temple-based Brahminism. As Zoya Hasan notes, state-led reforms often reflect "penal populism" directed at minorities rather than principled social transformation.[194]

This selective reformism reveals the Indian state's deeper investment in cultural nationalism and its reluctance to confront caste hierarchy. By enshrining the religious identity of Hindus in public life—be it through the construction of the Ram Mandir in Ayodhya or the celebration of Kumbh Melas as national spectacles—the state reinforces upper-caste dominance in both civic and religious spaces. Christophe Jaffrelot has argued that Hindu nationalism has effectively taken over the public sphere, with state patronage legitimizing Brahminical religiosity as national heritage.[195] Dalit religious forms, such as Bhakti poetry, Buddhist rites, or folk deities like Chokhamela or Mahadeo Koli, are rarely granted the same status.

This alignment of secularism with majoritarian interests has profound consequences for Dalit politics. It fragments Dalit identity along religious lines, making it difficult to forge cross-religious solidarity among oppressed castes. A Dalit Christian is denied SC status, while a Dalit Hindu is eligible; a Dalit Muslim is excluded from political representation, while a Buddhist convert retains it. This segmentation weakens the collective bargaining power of Dalits and incentivizes their co-optation into Hindu social structures.

Moreover, it delegitimizes conversion as a political act. Dr. Ambedkar, in leading the mass conversion to Buddhism in 1956, framed the move not merely as a spiritual transformation but as a rejection of the caste-based Hindu order. His message was unambiguous: Hinduism, with its graded inequality, was beyond reform; only religious exit could offer self-respect. Yet the Indian secular framework has made such exits costly. Converts lose access to reservations, face social ostracism, and are accused of communal motives. The state thus ensures that the "freedom of religion" guaranteed under Article 25 is constrained by the threat of economic and social penalty.

Anti-caste scholars have drawn attention to how Indian secularism serves not to dismantle caste but to administer it.[196] The administrative logic is also visible in how caste is managed through welfare rather than transformed through justice. Dalit struggles are reduced to demands for reservations or subsidies, never recognized as critiques of the foundational social order. The state treats caste not as a system of graded human dignity but as an identity category to be counted, accommodated, and contained. Meanwhile, upper-caste Hindu practices are depoliticized and rebranded as cultural legacy.

This transformation of secularism into a statist theology—where the state decides which religious expressions are acceptable and which are subversive—has rendered Dalit emancipation conditional, partial, and precarious. It offers legal recognition without substantive liberation, rights without dignity, and quotas without transformation. It disciplines Dalit aspiration through legal ambiguity and social exclusion, while legitimizing upper-caste dominance through cultural accommodation.

Indian secularism must be understood not as a normative commitment to equality but as a regime of governance that manages religious difference while preserving caste hierarchy. Its triadic structure—of equal respect, principled distance, and selective intervention—is operationalized not through justice but through control. For Dalits, this has meant perpetual marginality: denied the right to fully exit Hinduism, denied the right to equality within it, and denied the right to a secularism that acknowledges their full humanity.

Indian secularism, far from being neutral, has been designed in a way that protects the Hindu social order, especially caste hierarchy, while punishing Dalits who leave Hinduism. Dalits who convert to Islam or Christianity lose reservation benefits and legal protections, creating a perverse incentive structure that discourages exit from Hinduism and treats caste oppression as a purely "internal Hindu problem." This fiction not only legitimizes the idea that caste disappears upon conversion but also denies converted Dalits recognition of their continued marginalization. The result is a deliberate fracture: Hindu Dalits are categorized as Scheduled Castes with state-backed benefits, while Muslim and Christian Dalits are excluded and rendered invisible. This division destroys the possibility of a unified Dalit political identity and isolates converted Dalits, weakening any cross-religious solidarity that could threaten Brahminical dominance. At the same time, Hindu Dalits, tied to Hindu identity for material survival and repeatedly told that minorities are competitors or undeserving beneficiaries, become vulnerable to majoritarian mobilization. Hindutva forces exploit this dependency by portraying Muslims and Christians as threats, enabling the political deployment of Hindu Dalits as foot soldiers in communal conflicts against communities that share their history of caste oppression. In effect, Indian secularism preserves the caste hierarchy by keeping Dalits within Hinduism without dismantling the structures that subordinate them, offering minimal compensations to manage dissent while ensuring their continued availability as a loyal reservoir for Hindu political consolidation. Instead of separating religion and state, this model of secularism serves Hindu majoritarian interests, strengthens caste oppression, fragments Dalits, and weaponizes a section of them against others, deepening both caste domination and communal polarization.

The Architecture of Impunity

The Indian Constitution, while celebrated for its enumeration of fundamental rights and its commitment to social justice, also contains within it a deep contradiction—a set of provisions that institutionalize impunity for state functionaries. These provisions, often justified as safeguards for executive efficiency or protection of state sovereignty, have over time morphed into legal shields that enable the state to act with near-complete disregard for accountability. When it comes to the marginalized—Dalits, Adivasis, religious minorities, and dissenters—this architecture of impunity reveals itself not as an aberration but as a central feature of India's constitutional order.

The most direct sources of this impunity lie in Articles 311, 312, and 33 to 35, which limit the scope of rights in relation to state functionaries, security forces, and public employment. For instance, Article 311 protects civil servants from dismissal or punitive action without due process. While ostensibly a procedural safeguard, it has been weaponized to prevent disciplinary action even in cases of grave dereliction—such as custodial deaths, unlawful detention, or the failure to file First Information Reports (FIRs) in atrocity cases under the Scheduled Castes and Scheduled Tribes (Prevention of Atrocities) Act, 1989. Despite Sections 4 and 4A of that act prescribing penalties for such omissions, convictions of public servants remain virtually nonexistent. The immunity has thus become structural, not incidental[197].

More foundationally, Article 13(3)(a) defines "law" to include "ordinances, orders, bye-laws, rules, regulations, notifications, custom or usage." This broad definition means that even executive orders with no legislative backing can enjoy constitutional legitimacy unless explicitly struck down. Combined with the state's power under Article 356 (president's rule) and Articles 352–360 (emergency provisions), this allows the central or state governments to govern by executive fiat, often outside the purview of judicial review, especially in matters designated as involving the "security of the state."

Perhaps the most notorious sources of institutionalized impunity are found in Articles 33 and 34, which permit

Parliament to restrict or suspend fundamental rights in the context of the armed forces or during martial law. Article 33 empowers Parliament to modify the application of fundamental rights to the armed forces, police, and intelligence agencies, effectively insulating them from legal scrutiny. This forms the constitutional basis for laws like the Armed Forces (Special Powers) Act (AFSPA), which grants blanket immunity to soldiers for actions—including killing—undertaken "in the line of duty." Judicial review of such actions has been limited by courts on grounds of "national interest," despite damning reports by bodies like the UN Human Rights Council, which has called AFSPA "a symbol of excessive state power and legal immunity[198]."

Similarly, Article 34, dealing with martial law, indemnifies both state and nonstate actors for actions taken during such a declaration. Though rarely invoked formally, this article's logic underpins many laws like the Disturbed Areas Act, where state repression is normalized through legal immunities. In effect, it grants retroactive legal cover to violence, especially in conflict zones populated predominantly by Adivasis and Muslims.

The Code of Criminal Procedure also embeds impunity. Section 197 of the Code of Criminal Procedure (CrPC) (Section 218 in the Bharatiya Nagarik Suraksha Sanhita) prohibits courts from taking cognizance of offenses allegedly committed by public servants "while acting or purporting to act in the discharge of official duty" without prior sanction from the government. This provision, which applies even to grave crimes like custodial torture and extrajudicial killings, has resulted in countless cases being dismissed or stalled for want of sanction. As Justice V. R. Krishna Iyer once lamented, Section 197 has become a "charter for bureaucratic despotism."[199]

This legal immunity extends to judges as well. Judges of the high courts and Supreme Court enjoy near-absolute immunity under Articles 121 and 124(4), with removal requiring an elaborate impeachment process. While such insulation is necessary to protect judicial independence, it has created a climate where judicial inaction, caste bias, or failure to act in cases involving state atrocities can proceed unchecked. This is especially true in cases where lower courts summarily dismiss atrocity cases or grant bail in egregious hate crimes, further emboldening perpetrators and alienating victims.

Importantly, the doctrine of sovereign immunity, inherited from colonial jurisprudence, continues to haunt the Indian legal system. While the Supreme Court in *Nilabati Behera v. State of Orissa* (AIR 1993 SC 1960) attempted to pierce this veil by awarding compensation in a custodial death case, such cases remain exceptions. The more prevalent reality is reflected in *Kartar Singh v. State of Punjab* (AIR 1994 SC 1800), where the Court upheld the validity of TADA (Terrorist and Disruptive Activities [Prevention] Act), accepting the state's argument for extreme measures despite overwhelming evidence of misuse against minorities and Dalits.

Constitutional silence also contributes to this problem. Nowhere in the Constitution is there a positive obligation on the state to punish its own officials for rights violations. Rights are framed as negative liberties—freedom from interference—rather than positive entitlements that the state must secure. This has created a perverse asymmetry, where the state is both violator and judge of its own violations. Victims of state violence must rely on writ petitions, public interest litigation, or National Human Rights Commission interventions, none of which offer binding or immediate relief. The state, meanwhile, acts as both executioner and arbiter.

It is in this context that the idea of "rule of law" in India must be interrogated. For large sections of the population—especially Dalits and Adivasis—the law is not a shield but a sword. It is invoked selectively, applied disproportionately, and enforced with impunity. Legal protections for officials who commit atrocities and systemic nonimplementation of accountability provisions have converted the Constitution's promises into instruments of betrayal.

The call for legal reform, therefore, must move beyond procedural tinkering. It must begin by acknowledging the caste and class nature of impunity in India. Until public servants are held criminally liable for failing to protect citizens—particularly those from historically oppressed groups—the Constitution will continue to be a document of selective justice. A democratic republic cannot endure on the back of impunity. It must instead find its strength in the uncompromising pursuit of accountability, especially from those who wield power in its name.

A Constitutional Betrayal of the Marginalised

A primary source of this impunity is Article 22, which legitimizes preventive detention even without trial. While the Constituent Assembly witnessed significant opposition to preventive detention by members like H. V. Kamath, K. T. Shah, and Thakur Das Bhargava, the article was retained with minimal safeguards. This provision, inherited from colonial rule, continues to be abused disproportionately against marginalized communities. The National Security Act (NSA) and Unlawful Activities (Prevention) Act (UAPA)—both legal progeny of preventive detention—allow detention without charge for extended periods, reverse the presumption of innocence, and render bail virtually unattainable. Data from the National Crime Records Bureau (NCRB) and studies by the People's Union for Civil Liberties (PUCL) consistently reveal that Muslims, Dalits, and Adivasis form a grossly disproportionate share of detainees under such laws.

The institutional mechanisms meant to redress or prevent atrocities often function as shields for state impunity. The Scheduled Castes and Scheduled Tribes (Prevention of Atrocities) Act, 1989—enacted to curb caste-based violence—

mandates immediate FIR registration, speedy investigation, and special courts. However, these provisions are routinely ignored. A 2020 study by the National Dalit Movement for Justice (NDMJ) showed that in over 40 percent of atrocity cases, FIRs were not filed, and in 70 percent of cases, the police failed to complete investigation within the prescribed time. Conviction rates under the act remain abysmally low (just 32 percent for SCs and 26 percent for STs in 2021, per NCRB), not due to false complaints—as claimed by dominant caste groups—but because of poor investigation, intimidation of witnesses, and collusion between the police, prosecutors, and accused. Despite Section 4 of the act penalizing public servants for dereliction of duty, no police officer or magistrate has ever been convicted for failing to act in atrocity cases.

The CrPC and Indian Penal Code (IPC) also contain provisions that shield state agents. Under Section 197 of the CrPC, no public servant can be prosecuted for actions "done in the discharge of official duty" without prior government sanction—a clause weaponized to block judicial scrutiny in cases of custodial torture or fake encounters. In *Extra Judicial Execution Victim Families Association (EEVFAM) v. Union of India* (2016), the Supreme Court, while hearing a case involving 1,528 alleged fake encounters in Manipur, recognized the abuse of such laws. Yet convictions remain elusive.

Even international bodies have recognized the widespread

abuse of power. The UN Working Group on Arbitrary Detention (WGAD), in its 2022 opinion on the detention of Kashmiri politician Waheed Para, noted that Indian authorities routinely use vague anti-terror laws like the UAPA to silence dissent. Similarly, Amnesty International India, before its forced shutdown in 2020, published detailed reports documenting the arbitrary detention, torture, and custodial deaths of Dalits and Muslims across Uttar Pradesh and Chhattisgarh. Human Rights Watch, in its 2021 report, highlighted police brutality in India's tribal belts, noting that Adivasi villagers are routinely branded Maoists and subjected to extrajudicial killings without evidence. A virtual genocide has been going on against Adivasis and Dalits for over the last four decades in the name of ending the Maoist insurgency, without any attempt ever to understand their grievances. There is no more hiding the intent that the state wants to hand over mineral-rich lands under their habitats to corporate plunder.

Regional examples further underscore how impunity plays out on the ground. In Jharkhand, the death of Munda tribal youth Rupesh Tirkey in 2019, allegedly in custody, led to no action against the police despite glaring inconsistencies in official accounts. In Tamil Nadu, Jayaraj and Bennix, two Dalit men, were brutally tortured to death in police custody in 2020. Public outrage led to temporary suspensions, but convictions have yet to materialize. In Chhattisgarh's Bastar region, thousands of Adivasis have been arrested over the past two decades as alleged Maoists—without evidence, trial, or legal aid. In the case of Soni Sori, an Adivasi schoolteacher turned activist, police stripped her, inserted stones into her private parts, and later fabricated cases against her. Not one officer was punished.

What emerges from this pattern is not merely a failure of justice but a state policy of governance through fear and selective violence. Draconian laws are applied selectively—rarely against corporate violators or political elites, but often against dissenters, students, Adivasi villagers, Dalit protestors, and Muslim activists. Judicial silence—or worse, endorsement—of this pattern has led to a de facto suspension of constitutional morality. As legal scholar Ujjwal Kumar Singh writes, India's legal system legitimizes state illegality through procedural formalism that masks violence as law enforcement.[200]

The structural impunity is further entrenched by the absence of institutional memory. Commissions of inquiry—such as the Justice Srikrishna Commission on the 1992 Mumbai riots or the Justice Reddy Commission on encounter killings—submit damning reports, but their recommendations are rarely acted upon. The bureaucracy, judiciary, and police retain a culture of impunity, backed by political patronage and institutional inertia.

The Indian state's impunity is not incidental but systemic—rooted in the very Constitution, protected by legal frameworks, and normalized through judicial and political practice. For Dalits, Adivasis, and Muslims, this impunity translates into routine terror, incarceration, and erasure. The ideals of liberty, equality, and dignity remain distant dreams—betrayed not by enemies of the state but by the state itself.

A Virtual Police State

Over the decades, India has witnessed a steady transformation into a police state, where the coercive arm of the state functions with near-total impunity. The police, envisaged as a neutral institution tasked with protecting the public and maintaining law and order, has mutated into a political instrument wielded by those in power. A thick and enduring nexus has emerged between political elites and the police bureaucracy, wherein the latter acts as an enforcer of the former's interests—ranging from electoral manipulation and suppression of dissent to shielding illicit financial and criminal activities. This perverse alliance has led to a situation where those who question or resist this arrangement—be they journalists, activists, students, or local communities—are immediately branded as threats to "public order," "national security," or, in the now fashionable term, "urban Naxals." The idea of the rule of law becomes hollow when the police can frame, torture, incarcerate, and even eliminate individuals with fabricated charges, confident that accountability mechanisms are, at best, symbolic.

At the heart of this police state lies a structural impunity facilitated not only by executive inaction but by judicial complicity. Custodial torture, deaths in lockups, prolonged incarceration without charge, and even fake encounters are no longer aberrations but part of the accepted repertoire of statecraft. While the most dramatic illustration of this is the staged encounter—often celebrated by sections of the media and political class as "justice delivered"—the more routine and insidious damage is caused by fabricated FIRs, manipulated evidence, and endless pretrial detentions, particularly under draconian laws like UAPA, NSA, and AFSPA. The Indian judiciary, which ought to have been the bulwark against this degeneration, has largely abdicated its constitutional responsibility. Bail—ostensibly a right—is increasingly treated as a privilege. As a result, the republic has become a battleground where the state appears to be at war with its own people, and where Dalits, Adivasis, and Muslims are the most frequent casualties—not merely because of their identities, but because their marginality makes them expendable in the eyes of a majoritarian, security-obsessed state.

EPILOGUE

The Burden of a Text

The foregoing chapters have attempted to pierce through the sentimental and ideological fog that enshrouds the Indian Constitution, particularly in its presumed role as a charter of social justice for Dalits. Contrary to its popular and almost sacred perception—both in dominant political discourse and among Dalits themselves—this text has sought to foreground the Constitution's deep structural silences, its moral evasions, and its accommodation of oppressive continuities. Among Dalits, the Constitution commands not only reverence but emotional investment, often mediated through the towering figure of Dr. Ambedkar, who is widely held to be its chief architect and their liberator. This veneration, however, rarely rests on a critical assessment of the document's contents or its historical function; instead, it draws sustenance from the symbolic elevation of Ambedkar and his perceived imprint on its liberal-democratic soul.

Yet the historical record reveals a more complex story. Ambedkar, who entered the Constituent Assembly through an eleventh-hour political arrangement—having earlier been excluded from electoral access to it—was made chairman of the Drafting Committee not by accident but arguably as part of a larger Gandhian strategy. In this telling, Ambedkar's inclusion served to bind Dalits emotionally to a constitutional project that otherwise bore the unmistakable imprint of the Congress oligarchy. As I have hypothesized elsewhere, it was perhaps only Gandhi who possessed the political foresight to see that symbolic representation could perform the work of pacification.[201] Once inducted, Ambedkar, despite his well-known opposition to the Congress's duplicities and his trenchant critique of caste Hinduism, was bound by party discipline as a member of the Congress Assembly Party. He was thus compelled to defend policies and positions scripted by the Congress oligarchy—many of which have been discussed in the preceding pages. In moments of candor, Ambedkar himself confessed the compromise.

During the discussions over the Andhra State Bill, 1953, on 2 September 1953, Ambedkar said: "People always keep on saying to me: 'Oh, you are the maker of the Constitution.' My answer is I was a hack. What I was asked to do, I did much against my will[202]." When M. S. Ranawat, a member from Rajasthan, reminded him that he defended it, he retorted: "We lawyers defend many things."[203] He further elaborated: "Sir, my friends tell me that I have made the Constitution.

But I am quite prepared to say that I shall be the first person to burn it out. I do not want it. It does not suit anybody. But, whatever that may be, if our people want to carry on, they must not forget that there are majorities and there are minorities, and they simply cannot ignore the minorities by saying, 'Oh, no. To recognise you is to harm democracy.'"[204]

Two years later, during the discussions on the Constitution (Fourth Amendment) Bill, 1954, in response to Dr. Anup Singh, a member from Punjab, who reminded him of his remark that he would burn the Constitution, Ambedkar replied: "We built a temple for a god to come in and reside, but before the god could be installed, if the devil had taken possession of it, what else could we do except destroy the temple? We did not intend that it should be occupied by the Asuras. We intended it to be occupied by the devas. That is the reason why I said I would rather like to burn it."[205]

It was no answer. Perhaps Ambedkar realized the futility of disowning the past and tried to offer a more measured response. Yet his statement was not entirely without conviction, for he did hold the view that even a bad constitution could work well if implemented by good people, and a good constitution could fail if those entrusted with it were bad. What he meant by good or bad people, however, was the presence or absence of "constitutional morality." But the question does not end there. Constitutional morality does not emerge from a vacuum; it is, arguably, a task of the Constitution itself to cultivate it, first among the people who are to operate the Constitution and then among the larger mass of citizens.

Without venturing further into that normative terrain, it is important to note that the popular association of the Constitution with Ambedkar's emancipatory philosophy is erroneous. It is a ploy by the ruling classes. The Constitution was a product shaped by the political priorities of the Congress-dominated Constituent Assembly. And the Assembly was primarily composed of the landed elite, emergent bourgeoisie, and Western-educated upper-caste intelligentsia. Far from being a radical blueprint for social justice, the Constitution emerged as a consensus document reflecting the interests of these dominant social strata, with Ambedkar constrained to play the role of draftsman rather than free architect.

Even if Ambedkar had complete freedom, whether he could have drafted a radically different Constitution remains speculative. His proposal in *The State and Minorities*—which advocated nationalization of land, promotion of cooperative farming, state control over key industries, and universal life insurance—suggests a more redistributive and socialist orientation. However, it did not go far enough in obligating the state to provide the foundational conditions for real equality: universal and free access to quality education, health care, and livelihood security. Without these guarantees, even his progressive economic vision fell short of a comprehensive agenda for mass empowerment. Moreover, these goals clashed with the continued protection of private property rights, limiting their feasibility within the prevailing political framework.

Perhaps the Constitution could not have been very different from what it is. After all, it emerged from the prevailing balance of class forces—a codification of the dominant class's interests into law. A constitution cannot stand above society; it embodies the political will of those who hold power. For it to genuinely serve the interests of Dalits, it is incumbent upon them to shape their politics in a way that compels the ruling classes to respond. There can be no messianic solution—only the hard work of collective political assertion.

Notes

1 George Grote, *A History of Greece: From the Time of Solon to 403 BC* (London and New York: Routledge, 1907/2001).

2 Archives—Constitution of India, 4 November 1948.

3 BAWS 13: 61.

4 Bombay: Government Press, 1857.

5 Candrasinhji Gholap, ed., *A Compendious Marathi–English Dictionary* (Bombay: Bombay Education Society, 1873).

6 BAWS 19: 365, 368, 373.

7 "Anna Bhau Sathe," Social Studies Foundation, 18 July 2024, https://socialstudiesfoundation.org/2024/07/18/anna-bhau-sathe/.

8 Baburao Bagul, "Dalit Sahitya: Aajche Krantividnyan (Dalit Literature: The Revolutionary Science of Today)," in *When I Hid My Caste: Stories by Baburao Bagul*, trans. Jerry Pinto (New Delhi: Speaking Tiger Books, 2009).

9 "Census Tables," *Census of India*, https://censusindia.gov.in/census.website/data/census-tables.

10 Oliver Mendelsohn and Marika Vicziany, *The Untouchables: Subordination, Poverty, and the State in Modern India* (Cambridge: Cambridge University Press, 1998), 72–89.

11 Gail Omvedt, *Dalits and the Democratic Revolution: Dr. Ambedkar and the Dalit Movement in Colonial India* (New Delhi: Sage Publications, 1994), chap. 3.

12 Christophe Jaffrelot, *Dr. Ambedkar and Untouchability:*

Analysing and Fighting Caste (New York: Columbia University Press, 2005), 114.

13 Gopal Guru, "The Interface Between Ambedkar and the Dalit Cultural Movement," in *The Cracked Mirror: An Indian Debate on Experience and Theory*, ed. Gopal Guru and Sundar Sarukkai (New Delhi: Sage Publications, 2012), 45–47.

14 Badri Narayan, *The Politics of Forgotten Heroes: The Untold Story of Dalit Leaders in India* (New Delhi: Orient BlackSwan, 2011).

15 Rosalind O'Hanlon, *Caste, Conflict and Ideology: Mahatma Jotirao Phule and Low Caste Protest in Nineteenth-Century Western India* (Cambridge: Cambridge University Press, 1985), 83–88.

16 Eleanor Zelliot, *From Untouchable to Dalit: Essays on the Ambedkar Movement* (New Delhi: Manohar, 1992), 25–32.

17 Anand Teltumbde, *Republic of Caste: Thinking Equality in the Time of Neoliberal Hindutva* (New Delhi: Navayana, 2018), 61–66.

18 Bernard S. Cohn, *Colonialism and Its Forms of Knowledge: The British in India* (Princeton, NJ: Princeton University Press, 1996), 9–13.

19 Sumit Sarkar, *Modern India: 1885–1947* (Delhi: Macmillan, 1983), 29; Amiya P. Sen, *Rammohun Roy: A Critical Biography* (New Delhi: Penguin, 2012), 82–84.

20 Lynn Zastoupil, *Rammohun Roy and the Making of Victorian Britain* (Basingstoke: Palgrave, 2010), 95; Lata Mani, *Contentious Traditions: The Debate on Sati in Colonial India* (Berkeley: University of California Press, 1998), 115–20.

20 Arjun Appadurai, *Modernity at Large: Cultural Dimensions of Globalization* (Minneapolis: University of Minnesota Press, 1996), 115.

22 Mitra Sharafi, *Law and Identity in Colonial South Asia: Parsi Legal Culture, 1772–1947* (Cambridge: Cambridge University Press, 2014), 111–13.

23 David Omissi, *The Sepoy and the Raj: The Indian Army, 1860–1940* (Basingstoke: Macmillan, 1994), 27–29.

24 Nicholas B. Dirks, *Castes of Mind: Colonialism and the Making of Modern India* (Princeton, NJ: Princeton University Press, 2001), 10–13, 202–5.

25 "RSS mouthpiece Panchjanya defends caste system," *Dhanam English*, quoting editorial on missionaries and 'divide and rule' policy, https://english.dhanamonline.com/personalities/rss-mouthpiece-defends-caste-system-it-unified-india-6847219/.

26 Christophe Jaffrelot, *India's Silent Revolution: The Rise of the Lower Castes in North India* (London: C. Hurst & Co., 2003), 13–18.

27 Eleanor Zelliot, *From Untouchable to Dalit: Essays on the Ambedkar Movement* (New Delhi: Manohar, 2005), 25–28.

28 David Omissi, *The Sepoy and the Raj: The Indian Army, 1860–1940* (Basingstoke: Macmillan, 1994), 20–24.

29 Chinnaiah Jangam, *Dalits and the Making of Modern India* (New Delhi: Oxford University Press, 2017), 85–88.

30 Christophe Jaffrelot, *India's Silent Revolution: The Rise of the Lower Castes in North India* (London: C. Hurst & Co., 2003), 23–27.

31 B. R. Ambedkar, "Speech at Mahad," in *Dr. Babasaheb Ambedkar: Writings and Speeches*, vol. 2, ed. Vasant Moon (Bombay: Education Department, Government of Maharashtra, 1982), 254.

32 Susan Bayly, *Caste, Society and Politics in India from the Eighteenth Century to the Modern Age* (Cambridge: Cambridge University Press, 1999), esp. 225–50.

33 P. Sanal Mohan, "Ayyankali: A Dalit Leader of Organic Protest," in *The Political Economy of Protest and Patience: East European and Indian Perspectives*, ed. (New Delhi: Sage, 2015).

34 Soli J. Sorabjee, "Rights and Human Rights in the Modern World: The Experience of Working the Bill of Rights in the

Indian Constitution," in *The Future of Liberal Democracy*, ed. Robert Fatton and R. K. Ramazani (New York: Palgrave Macmillan, 2004), https://doi.org/10.1057/9781403981455_8.

35 Marc Galanter, *Competing Equalities: Law and the Backward Classes in India* (Berkeley: University of California Press, 1984), 118–20.

36 Anand Teltumbde, *Mahad: The Making of the First Dalit Revolt* (New Delhi: Aakar Books, 2016), 126–30.

37 Christophe Jaffrelot, *Dr. Ambedkar and Untouchability: Fighting the Indian Caste System* (New York: Columbia University Press, 2005), 35–38.

38 B. R. Ambedkar, *Annihilation of Caste* (1936), in *Dr. Babasaheb Ambedkar: Writings and Speeches*, vol. 1 (BAWS 1: 25–30).

39 Eleanor Zelliot, *From Untouchable to Dalit: Essays on the Ambedkar Movement* (New Delhi: Manohar, 1992), 45.

40 M. S. S. Pandian, "One Step Outside Modernity: Caste, Identity Politics and Public Sphere," *Economic and Political Weekly* 37, no. 18 (2002): 1735–41.

41 Anupama Rao, *The Caste Question: Dalits and the Politics of Modern India* (Berkeley: University of California Press, 2009), 141–43.

42 B. R. Ambedkar, *Evidence before the First Round Table Conference*, in *Dr. Babasaheb Ambedkar: Writings and Speeches*, vol. 2, 489–510.

43 Ravinder Kumar, *The Making of a Nation: Essays in Indian History and Politics* (New Delhi: Manohar, 1989), 122–25.

44 B. R. Ambedkar, "Statement at the Second Round Table Conference," in *Dr. Babasaheb Ambedkar: Writings and Speeches*, vol. 2, 526–30.

45 Government of India, *Communal Award* (White Paper, 1932); see also Galanter, *Competing Equalities*, 130–32.

46 Dhananjay Keer, *Dr. Ambedkar: Life and Mission* (Bombay: Popular Prakashan, 1954), 184–90.

47 Eleanor Zelliot, *From Untouchable to Dalit: Essays on the Ambedkar Movement* (New Delhi: Manohar, 1992), 49–51.
48 B. R. Ambedkar, "The Poona Pact," in BAWS 9: 13–18.
49 Government of India, *Government of India Act, 1935*; see also Rajeev Bhargava, "Political Secularism: Why It Is Needed and What Can Be Learnt from Its Indian Version," in *Secularism and Its Critics*, ed. Rajeev Bhargava (Delhi: Oxford University Press, 1998), 498–503.
50 "Speech to the Scheduled Castes Federation, 6 May 1945," *Indian Annual Register* (JARI), 1946, vol. 1, 321–24.
51 Granville Austin, *The Indian Constitution: Cornerstone of a Nation* (Oxford: Clarendon Press, 1966), 10.
52 Ibid. p. 11.
53 Ibid, p. 19.
54 S. Gopal, ed., *Selected Works of Jawaharlal Nehru*, vol. 2 (New Delhi: Jawaharlal Nehru Memorial Fund, 2003), 805.
55 Susan Billington Harper, *In the Shadow of the Mahatma: Bishop V. S. Azariah and the Travails of Christianity in India* (Abingdon: Routledge, 2019), 131.
56 *Constituent Assembly Debates, Official Report, vol. 7, 4 November 1948, 31–44; BAWS 13: 60.*
57 Letter from Rajendra Prasad to B. G. Kher, prime minister of Bombay, 30 June 1947, Prasad Papers.
58 Archives—Constitution of India, CAD, 29 April 1947, para 3.18.30.
59 Archives—Constitution of India, CAD, 29 April 1947, para 3.18.99.
60 Archives—Constitution of India, CAD, 29 April 1947, para 3.18.103.
61 CAD, 22 November 1949, para 11.162.116, Constitution of India, https://www.constitutionofindia.net/debates/22-nov-1949/.
62 CAD, 22 November 1949, para 11.162.166, Constitution

of India, https://www.constitutionofindia.net/debates/22-nov-1949/.

63 CAD, 22 November 1949, para 7.51.80, Constitution of India, https://www.constitutionofindia.net/debates/22-nov-1949/

64 CAD, 29 November 1948, para 7.62.164, Constitution of India, https://www.constitutionofindia.net/debates/29-nov-1948/.

65 CAD, 29 November 1948, para 7.62.168, Constitution of India, https://www.constitutionofindia.net/debates/29-nov-1948/.

66 CAD, 29 November 1948, para 7.62.173, Constitution of India, https://www.constitutionofindia.net/debates/29-nov-1948/.

67 CAD, 29 November 1948, para 7.62.175, Constitution of India, https://www.constitutionofindia.net/debates/29-nov-1948/.

68 CAD, 29 November 1948, para 7.62.177, Constitution of India, https://www.constitutionofindia.net/debates/29-nov-1948/.

69 "Understanding Untouchability: A Comprehensive Study of Practices and Conditions in 1589 Villages," Navsarjan Trust and Robert F. Kennedy Center for Justice and Human Rights, http://navsarjan.org/Documents/Untouchability_Report_FINAL_Complete.pdf.

70 Child Rights International Network (CRIN), archive, archive.crin.org.

71 Child Rights International Network (CRIN), archive, archive.crin.org.

72 "Biggest caste survey: One in four Indians admit to practising untouchability," *The Indian Express*, https://indianexpress.com/.

73 "Caste Survey Data Tables," drupal-base-s3-drupalshareds3-1qwpjwcnqwwsr.s3.amazonaws.com

74 "Caste Survey Data Tables," drupal-base-s3-drupalshareds3-1qwpjwcnqwwsr.s3.amazonaws.com.
75 "Caste Survey Data Tables," drupal-base-s3-drupalshareds3-1qwpjwcnqwwsr.s3.amazonaws.com.
76 "Caste Survey Data Tables," drupal-base-s3-drupalshareds3-1qwpjwcnqwwsr.s3.amazonaws.com.
77 Anand Teltumbde, "Dalits under the Modi Raj," in *Whither Human Rights in India?*, ed. Anand Teltumbde (Gurugram: Penguin, 2025), 287.
78 "Rajasthan: Dalit boy beaten to death for 'touching' water pot," *Times of India* (Jodhpur edition), 14 August 2022, https://timesofindia.indiatimes.com/city/jodhpur/rajasthan-dalit-boy-beaten-to-death-by-teacher-for-touching-water-pot/articleshow/93549744.cms.
79 "How dare you touch it? Dalit student in UP thrashed by teacher for touching water bottle," *Observer Post*, https://theobserverpost.com/how-dare-you-touch-it-dalit-student-in-up-thrashed-by-teacher-for-touching-water-bottle/.
80 Dhananjay Keer, *Mahatma Gandhi: Political Saint and Unarmed Prophet* (Bombay: Popular Prakashan, 1973), 434–37.
81 Jawaharlal Nehru, *The Discovery of India* (New Delhi: Oxford University Press, 1981; orig. 1946), 374–78.
82 Christophe Jaffrelot, *India's Silent Revolution: The Rise of the Lower Castes in North India* (London: Hurst, 2003), 9–14.
83 Eleanor Zelliot, "Dr. Ambedkar and the Search for a Meaningful Buddhism," in S. J. Tambiah, ed., *Buddhism and the Spirit of the New Humanism* (Paris: UNESCO, 1983), 163–77.
84 Gail Omvedt, *Dalits and the Democratic Revolution: Dr. Ambedkar and the Dalit Movement in Colonial India* (New Delhi: Sage, 1994), 212–14.
85 Marc Galanter, *Competing Equalities: Law and the Backward Classes in India* (Berkeley: University of California Press, 1984), 16–20.

86 Government of India, *The Scheduled Castes Order, 1936.*

87 Nicholas B. Dirks, *Castes of Mind: Colonialism and the Making of Modern India* (Princeton, NJ: Princeton University Press, 2001), 9–11.

88 Partha Chatterjee, *Nationalist Thought and the Colonial World: A Derivative Discourse?* (Delhi: Oxford University Press, 1986), 115–18.

89 Anand Teltumbde, "Dalits under the Modi Raj," in *Whither Human Rights in India?*, ed. Anand Teltumbde (Gurugram: Penguin, 2025), 281.

90 National Crime Records Bureau, "Table 7A.2," *Crime in India 2023*, https://www.ncrb.gov.in/uploads/nationalcrimerecords bureau/custom/1702027966TABLE 7A2.pdf.

91 Abhinay Lakshman, "In over 90% of sewer deaths, workers had no safety gear: Government audit," *The Hindu*, 23 July 2025.

92 "Pollution deaths and sewer workers," *Business Standard*, 31 July 2024.

93 Omkar Gokhale, "Total 81 people have died in the state due to manual scavenging, Maharashtra free of such practice: Govt tells HC," *Indian Express*, 1 July 2024.

94 Abhinay Lakshman, "In over 90% of sewer deaths, workers had no safety gear: government audit," *The Hindu*, 23 July 2025.

95 "Modern Slavery in India," Global Slavery Index, Walk Free Foundation, https://www.walkfree.org/global-slavery-index/country-studies/india/.

96 Thomas R. Metcalf, *Ideologies of the Raj* (Cambridge: Cambridge University Press, 1995), 44–46.

97 Bipan Chandra et al., *India's Struggle for Independence, 1857–1947* (New Delhi: Penguin Books, 1989), 525.

98 Francesca R. Jensenius, *Social Justice through Inclusion: The Consequences of Electoral Quotas in India* (New Delhi: Oxford University Press, 2017), 35–38.

99 Anand Teltumbde, *Iconoclast: A Reflective Biography of Dr Babasaheb Ambedkar* (Gurugram: Penguin, 2024), 192.

100 B. R. Ambedkar, *Evidence before the Southborough Committee*, BAWS 1: 263–65.

101 Ambar Sharma, "Reservations Can Take the Disadvantaged to Parliament, But Not into Key Positions," IndiaSpend, https://www.indiaspend.com/governance/reservation-scheduled-castes-tribes-representation-social-justice-755256.

102 Ambar Sharma, "Even in parliamentary committees, Scheduled Castes and Tribes have a limited voice," *Scroll.in*, https://scroll.in/article/997652/even-in-parliamentary-committees-scheduled-castes-and-tribes-have-a-limited-voice.

103 Robert Michels, *Political Parties: A Sociological Study of the Oligarchical Tendencies of Modern Democracy* (New York: Free Press, 1962; orig. 1911).

104 Antonio Gramsci, *Selections from the Prison Notebooks*, ed. and trans. Quintin Hoare and Geoffrey Nowell Smith (New York: International Publishers, 1971).

105 Frantz Fanon, *The Wretched of the Earth*, trans. Richard Philcox (New York: Grove Press, 2004).

106 Partha Chatterjee, *The Politics of the Governed: Reflections on Popular Politics in Most of the World* (New York: Columbia University Press, 2004).

107 Anand Teltumbde, *The Republic of Caste: Thinking Equality in the Time of Neoliberal Hindutva* (New Delhi: Navayana, 2018).

108 Francesca Refsum Jensenius, *Social Justice Through Inclusion: The Consequences of Electoral Quotas in India* (New Delhi: Oxford University Press, 2017); and Simon Chauchard, *Why Representation Matters: The Meaning of Ethnic Quotas in Rural India* (Cambridge: Cambridge University Press, 2017).

109 Francesca Refsum Jensenius, "Development from Representation? A Study of Quotas for the Scheduled Castes in India," *American Economic Journal: Applied Economics* 7, no. 3 (2015): 196–220.

110 Damodaram Sanjivayya was the first Dalit to become a Chief Minister, serving Andhra Pradesh from January 1960 to March

1962. Bhola Paswan Shastri held the position of Bihar's Chief Minister three times between 1968 and 1971, while Ram Sundar Das served as Bihar's CM from April 1979 to February 1980. Mayawati made history by becoming the Chief Minister of Uttar Pradesh four times (1995, 1997, 2002–2003, and 2007–2012), leading her own party, the Bahujan Samaj Party (BSP). Charanjit Singh Channi served as Punjab's CM from September 2021 to March 2022. Sushilkumar Shinde was Maharashtra's Chief Minister from 2003 to 2004, and Jitan Ram Manjhi held the post in Bihar from May 2014 to February 2015.

111 Kanshi Ram, *Chamcha Raj: An Era of Stooges* (New Delhi: self-published, 1982), http://ambedkar.org/research/The_Chamcha_Age.htm.

112 Royal Commission on Electoral Systems, *Report* (1910), Cmd. 5270, esp. 3–12.

113 Iain McLean, *What's Wrong with the British Constitution?* (Oxford: Oxford University Press, 2010), 78–81.

114 F. W. S. Craig, *Electoral Reform in Britain* (Newton Abbot: David & Charles, 1972), 45.

115 David Butler and Gareth Butler, *Twentieth-Century British Political Facts, 1900–2000* (London: Macmillan, 2000), 134.

116 Vernon Bogdanor, *The People and the Party System: The Referendum and Electoral Reform in British Politics* (Cambridge: Cambridge University Press, 1981), 96.

117 Abhay V. Datar, *Political Representation in India: Ideas and Contestations, 1908–1951* (New Delhi: Bloomsbury, 2019), 154.

118 Abhay V. Datar, *Political Representation in India: Ideas and Contestations, 1908–1951* (New Delhi: Bloomsbury, 2019), 155.

119 Abhay V. Datar, *Political Representation in India: Ideas and Contestations, 1908–1951* (New Delhi: Bloomsbury, 2019), 155.

120 Abhay V. Datar, *Political Representation in India: Ideas and Contestations, 1908–1951* (New Delhi: Bloomsbury, 2019), 156.

121 CAD, 17 July 1947, para 4.25.59–62, Constitution of India, https://www.constitutionofindia.net/debates/17-jul-1947/.

122 CAD, vol. 4 (28 July 1947).
123 CAD, 28 August 1947, para 5.44.117, Constitution of India, https://www.constitutionofindia.net/debates/28-aug-1947/.
124 CAD, 5 November 1948, para 7.49.143, Constitution of India, https://www.constitutionofindia.net/debates/05-nov-1948/.
125 CAD, 4 January 1949, para 7.79.33, Constitution of India, https://www.constitutionofindia.net/debates/04-jan-1949/.
126 CAD, 4 January 1949, para 7.79.98, Constitution of India, https://www.constitutionofindia.net/debates/04-jan-1949/.
127 CAD, 8 November 1948, para 7.51.54, Constitution of India, https://www.constitutionofindia.net/debates/08-nov-1948/.
128 CAD, 25 May 1949, para 8.91.73, Archives—Constitution of India; see also Constitution of India, https://www.constitutionofindia.net/debates/25-may-1949/.
129 https://www.constitutionofindia.net/debates/25-may-1949/.
130 CAD, 25 May 1949, para 7.79.176, Constitution of India, https://www.constitutionofindia.net/debates/25-may-1949/
131 CAD, 25 May 1949, para 7.52.61, Constitution of India, https://www.constitutionofindia.net/debates/25-may-1949/
132 CAD, 25 May 1949, para 7.52.89, Constitution of India, https://www.constitutionofindia.net/debates/25-may-1949/.
133 Abhay V. Datar, *Political Representation in India: Ideas and Contestations, 1908–1951* (New Delhi: Bloomsbury, 2019), 157.
134 CAD, 30 July 1949, para 9.107.142, Constitution of India, https://www.constitutionofindia.net/debates/30-jul-1949/.
135 CAD, 21 November 1949, para 11.161.17, Constitution of India, https://www.constitutionofindia.net/debates/21-nov-1949/
136 Archives—Constitution of India, *Constituent Assembly Debates*, 4 January 1949, para 7.79.185
137 Archives—Constitution of India, *Constituent Assembly Debates*, 4 January 1949, para 7.79.186; see also Abhay V. Datar, *Political Representation in India: Ideas and Contestations, 1908–1951* (New Delhi: Bloomsbury, 2019), 161

138 Archives—Constitution of India, *Constituent Assembly Debates*, 4 January 1949, para 7.79.189.

139 Abhay V. Datar, *Political Representation in India: Ideas and Contestations, 1908–1951* (New Delhi: Bloomsbury, 2019), 161

140 Abhay V. Datar, *Political Representation in India: Ideas and Contestations, 1908–1951* (New Delhi: Bloomsbury, 2019), 158.

141 Abhay V. Datar, *Political Representation in India: Ideas and Contestations, 1908–1951* (New Delhi: Bloomsbury, 2019), 158.

142 Abhay V. Datar, *Political Representation in India: Ideas and Contestations, 1908–1951* (New Delhi: Bloomsbury, 2019), 162.

143 Abhay V. Datar, *Political Representation in India: Ideas and Contestations, 1908–1951* (New Delhi: Bloomsbury, 2019), 209.

144 A CMS Report, *Poll Expenditure: The 2019 Elections*, https://www.cmsindia.org/sites/default/files/2019-05/Poll-Expenditure-the-2019-elections-cms-report.pdf.

145 Association for Democratic Reforms (ADR), "Criminals and Crorepatis? Meet the New MPs of Lok Sabha 2024," https://adrindia.org/content/criminals-and-crorepatis-meet-the-new-mps-of-lok-sabha-2024.

146 *"Poona Pact, 24 September 1932"*, BAWS 9: 383. Final clause: "The system of representation of Depressed Classes in the Public Services shall be on the same footing as that of other minorities... Every endeavour shall be made to secure fair representation..."

147 CAD, Vol. 7 (4 November 1948).

148 CAD, Vol. 7 (30 November 1948).

149 CAD, Vol. 7, 819.

150 CAD, Vol. 8 (25 May 1949).

151 CAD, Vol. 9 (17 August 1949).

152 CAD, Vol. 11 (22 November 1949).

153 CAD, Vol. 7 (November 1948).

154 CAD, Vol. 9 (25 August 1949).

155 CAD, Vol. 7 (November 1948).

156 CAD, Vol. 1, 66.

157 CAD, Vol. 1 (17 December 1946).
158 CAD, Vol. 7 (23 November 1948).
159 CAD, Vol. 7 (November 1948).
160 CAD, Vol. 9 (August 1949).
161 CAD (14 October 1949), speeches of Singh (9.122.70) and Nalavade (7.63.128).
162 CAD, Vol. 7, 701.
163 Marc Galanter, *Competing Equalities: Law and the Backward Classes in India* (Berkeley: University of California Press, 1984), 22, 25–30.
164 Christophe Jaffrelot, *India's Silent Revolution: The Rise of the Lower Castes in North India* (London: C. Hurst & Co., 2003), 233–36, 405–8.
165 *Constituent Assembly Debates*, Official Report, vol. 2, 407.
166 Christophe Jaffrelot, *India's Silent Revolution: The Rise of the Lower Castes in North India* (London: C. Hurst & Co., 2003), 405–8.
167 Marc Galanter, *Competing Equalities: Law and the Backward Classes in India* (Berkeley: University of California Press, 1984), 26–30.
168 Anand Teltumbde, *Republic of Caste: Thinking Equality in the Time of Neoliberal Hindutva* (New Delhi: Navayana, 2018), 36.
169 Anand Teltumbde, *Republic of Caste: Thinking Equality in the Time of Neoliberal Hindutva* (New Delhi: Navayana, 2018), 44.
170 Marc Galanter, *Competing Equalities: Law and the Backward Classes in India* (Berkeley: University of California Press, 1984), 25.
171 CAD, Vol. X, p. 243. 14 October 1949.
172 CAD, Vol. 7 (29 November 1948).
173 CAD, Vol. 7 (2 December 1948).
174 CAD, Vol. 5 (25 August 1947).
175 CAD, Vol. 7 (1 December 1948).
176 CAD, Vol. 7 (30 November 1948).

177 Christophe Jaffrelot, *Dr Ambedkar and Untouchability: Analysing and Fighting Caste* (New Delhi: Permanent Black, 2005), 127–29.
178 Marc Galanter, *Competing Equalities: Law and the Backward Classes in India* (Berkeley: University of California Press, 1984), 91.
179 George Jacob Holyoake, *The Principles of Secularism* (London: Austin & Co., 1871), https://ia902803.us.archive.org/33/items/theprinciplesofs36797gut/36797-h/36797-h.htm#link2HCH0003.
180 Rajeev Bhargava, "Political Secularism: Why It Is Needed and What Can Be Learnt from Its Indian Version," in *Secular States and Religious Diversity*, ed. Bruce Berman, Rajeev Bhargava, and André Laliberté (Vancouver: UBC Press, 2013), 11.
181 Archives—Constitution of India, CAD, 23 November 1949, para 11.163.150.
182 Archives—Constitution of India, CAD, 21 November 1949, para 10.151.48.
183 Archives—Constitution of India, CAD, 21 November 1949, para 11.161.16.
184 Archives—Constitution of India, CAD, 22 November 1949, para 11.162.31.
185 Archives—Constitution of India, CAD, 19 November 1949, para 11.160.79.
186 Archives—Constitution of India, CAD, 21 November 1949.
187 Archives—Constitution of India, CAD, 17 October 1949, para 10.154.534
188 Archives—Constitution of India, CAD, 15 November 1948, para 7.53.24.
189 Archives—Constitution of India, CAD, 15 November 1948, para 7.53.39.
190 Archives—Constitution of India, CAD, 15 November 1948, para 7.53.41.

191 Rajeev Bhargava, The Promise of India's Secular Democracy (New Delhi: Oxford University Press, 2010).

192 Ashis Nandy, Traditions, Tyranny and Utopias: Essays in the Politics of Awareness (New Delhi: Oxford University Press, 1987).

193 Faizan Mustafa, "The Hijab Case and the Indian Model of Secularism," *Indian Express*, March 2022.

194 Zoya Hasan, "Triple Talaq: Lawmaking as Political Messaging," *Economic and Political Weekly* 54, no. 32 (August 2019).

195 Christophe Jaffrelot, *Hindu Nationalism and the Politics of Fear* (New Delhi: Penguin, 2007).

196 Teesta Setalvad, "A Half Baked Secularism: Teesta Setalvad on Caste and Communalism," *Sabrang*, https://sabrangindia.in/half-baked-secularism-teesta-setalvad-caste-and-communalism/.

197 National Dalit Movement for Justice (NDMJ)–NCDHR, "Criminal Justice in the Shadow of Caste" (New Delhi, 2018), www.annihilatecaste.in/uploads/downloads/data_190118030229_21000.pdf.

198 UN Office of the High Commissioner for Human Rights (OHCHR), "Report of the Special Rapporteur on Extrajudicial, Summary or Arbitrary Executions," 2013, https://www.ohchr.org/en/special-procedures/sr-executions.

199 *State of Punjab v. Major Singh, AIR 1967 SC 63.*

200 Ujjwal Kumar Singh, *The State, Democracy and Anti-Terror Laws in India* (New Delhi: Sage, 2007).

201 Anand Teltumbde, *Iconoclast: A Reflective Biography of Dr Babasaheb Ambedkar* (Gurugram: Penguin, 2024), 338.

202 BAWS 15: 860.

203 Ibid.

204 Ibid., 862.

205 BAWS 15: 949.

www.ingramcontent.com/pod-product-compliance
Lightning Source LLC
Chambersburg PA
CBHW031348230926
51848CB00002B/430